DEADLY DISEASES AND EPIDEMICS

WHOOPING COUGH

DEADLY DISEASES AND EPIDEMICS

DEADLY DISEASES AND EPIDEMICS

WHOOPING COUGH

Patrick G. Guilfoile, Ph.D.

CONSULTING EDITOR
Hilary Babcock, M.D., M.P.H.,
Infectious Diseases Division,
Washington University School of Medicine,
Medical Director of Occupational Health (Infectious Diseases),
Barnes-Jewish Hospital and St. Louis Children's Hospital

FOREWORD BY
David Heymann
World Health Organization

CHELSEA HOUSE
PUBLISHERS
An imprint of Infobase Publishing

I thank my wife, Audrey, and my father, Thomas,
for their advice and assistance with this book.

Whooping Cough

Copyright © 2010 by Infobase Publishing

Chelsea House
An imprint of Infobase Publishing
132 West 31st Street
New York NY 10001

Library of Congress Cataloging-in-Publication Data

Guilfoile, Patrick
    Whooping cough / Patrick G. Guilfoile.
        p. cm. — (Deadly diseases and epidemics)
    Includes bibliographical references and index.
    ISBN-13: 978-1-60413-229-8 (hardcover : alk. paper)
    ISBN-10: 1-60413-229-9 (hardcover : alk. paper) 1. Whooping cough. I. Title. II. Series.

    RC204.G85 2010
    616.2'04—dc22   2009041340

Chelsea House books are available at special discounts when purchased in bulk
quantities for businesses, associations, institutions, or sales promotions. Please call our
Special Sales Department in New York at (212) 967-8800 or (800) 322-8755.

You can find Chelsea House on the World Wide Web at
http://www.chelseahouse.com

Text design by Terry Mallon
Cover design by Takeshi Takahashi
Composition by Mary Susan Ryan-Flynn
Cover printed by Bang Printing, Brainerd, Minn.
Book printed and bound by Bang Printing, Brainerd, Minn.
Date printed: May 2010
Printed in the United States of America

10 9 8 7 6 5 4 3 2 1

Table of Contents

Foreword

Communicable diseases kill and cause long-term disability. The microbial agents that cause them are dynamic, changeable, and resilient: They are responsible for more than 14 million deaths each year, mainly in developing countries.

Approximately 46 percent of all deaths in the developing world are due to communicable diseases, and almost 90 percent of these deaths are from AIDS, tuberculosis, malaria, and acute diarrheal and respiratory infections of children. In addition to causing great human suffering, these high-mortality communicable diseases have become major obstacles to economic development. They are a challenge to control either because of the lack of effective vaccines, or because the drugs that are used to treat them are becoming less effective because of antimicrobial drug resistance.

Millions of people, especially those who are poor and living in developing countries, are also at risk from disabling communicable diseases such as polio, leprosy, lymphatic filariasis, and onchocerciasis. In addition to human suffering and permanent disability, these communicable diseases create an economic burden—both on the workforce that handicapped persons are unable to join, and on their families and society, upon which they must often depend for economic support.

Finally, the entire world is at risk of the unexpected communicable diseases, those that are called emerging or re-emerging infections. Infection is often unpredictable because risk factors for transmission are not understood, or because it often results from organisms that cross the species barrier from animals to humans. The cause is often viral, such as Ebola and Marburg hemorrhagic fevers and severe acute respiratory syndrome (SARS). In addition to causing human suffering and death, these infections place health workers at great risk and are costly to economies. Infections such as Bovine Spongiform Encephalopathy (BSE) and the associated new human variant of Creutzfeldt-Jakob disease (vCJD) in Europe, and avian influenza A (H5N1) in Asia, are reminders of the seriousness of emerging and re-emerging infections. In addition, many of these infections have the potential to cause pandemics, which are a constant threat to our economies and public health security.

Science has given us vaccines and anti-infective drugs that have helped keep infectious diseases under control. Nothing demonstrates the effectiveness of vaccines better than the successful eradication of smallpox, the decrease in polio as the eradication program continues, and the decrease in measles when routine immunization programs are supplemented by mass vaccination campaigns.

Likewise, the effectiveness of anti-infective drugs is clearly demonstrated through prolonged life or better health in those infected with viral diseases such as AIDS, parasitic infections such as malaria, and bacterial infections such as tuberculosis and pneumococcal pneumonia.

But current research and development is not filling the pipeline for new anti-infective drugs as rapidly as resistance is developing, nor is vaccine development providing vaccines for some of the most common and lethal communicable diseases. At the same time, providing people with access to existing anti-infective drugs, vaccines, and goods such as condoms or bed nets—necessary for the control of communicable diseases in many developing countries—remains a great challenge.

Education, experimentation, and the discoveries that grow from them are the tools needed to combat high mortality infectious diseases, diseases that cause disability, or emerging and re-emerging infectious diseases. At the same time, partnerships between developing and industrialized countries can overcome many of the challenges of access to goods and technologies. This book may inspire its readers to set out on the path of drug and vaccine development, or on the path to discovering better public health technologies by applying our current understanding of the human genome and those of various infectious agents. Readers may likewise be inspired to help ensure wider access to those protective goods and technologies. Such inspiration, with pragmatic action, will keep us on the winning side of the struggle against communicable diseases.

David L. Heymann
Assistant Director General
Health Security and Environment
Representative of the Director General for Polio Eradication
World Health Organization
Geneva, Switzerland

1

What Is Whooping Cough?

A baby boy, who had been born in France three months prematurely, was hospitalized for chronic lung problems. After about four months of care in the hospital, he developed severe coughing fits. The infant was put into neonatal intensive care and diagnosed with whooping cough. Following treatment with the antibiotic josamycin, his condition quickly improved to the point that he was returned to the regular neonatal unit. Two days later he again developed a severe cough and was taken back into intensive care. This time he was treated with a different antibiotic, azithromycin, and after five days of treatment, he recovered. He remained hospitalized for another four months, but had no further bouts of whooping cough. His mother had developed a mild cough after the boy was born, and diagnostic tests indicated that she was infected with Bordetella pertussis, *the bacterium that causes whooping cough. It was likely that she was the source of the infection for her son. Following treatment with an antibiotic, the mother's cough abated. This case study illustrates several key points about whooping cough. The disease is most serious in infants. Adolescents and adults, who may have a mild case of whooping cough, frequently transmit the illness to the very young. The bacterium is normally susceptible to antibiotics, but antibiotic resistance is a growing concern. This case study was from 2006, showing that whooping cough is still a problem, even in developed countries.*[1]

Whooping cough is a serious **infectious** disease characterized by severe coughing fits. These coughing spells can be so prolonged and intense that the afflicted person has difficulty breathing. The name of the disease comes from this spasmodic, continuous coughing, which results in an intense inhalation after an episode, producing a whooping sound. Because of the intensity of the coughing fits, a person with whooping cough will frequently vomit after a coughing fit, and may develop a blue pallor due to the lack of oxygen during coughing bouts.

The course of the illness is frequently prolonged. The disease starts with mild symptoms—a runny nose, sneezing, sore throat, inflamed eyes, mild cough—usually about one week after the initial infection (although the symptoms may appear anywhere from five days to three weeks after infection). At this stage fever is uncommon and the cough is initially nonproductive (no phlegm is brought up). About two weeks following the initial symptoms, the cough becomes more severe. This intense stage of coughing typically lasts about two weeks and gradually abates over one to two months. Often, between coughing spells, the patient will not show much sign of illness. Coughing fits are more frequent at night, and can be triggered by exposure to a number of different stimuli such as a sudden noise or eating or drinking.[2] Secondary infections in the lungs are common, as *Bordetella pertussis* destroys **ciliated cells** in the respiratory tract that naturally protect against infections. Other complications associated with whooping cough include ear infections, nosebleeds, and bruising. In cases with very severe coughing, hernias can develop, the retinas in the eyes can detach, and the pressure in the skull can increase to the point where blood vessels in the brain rupture.[3]

Whooping cough occurs in infants who are too young to be vaccinated, and in young children who are unvaccinated. The disease, often in a mild form, is also occurring with greater frequency in adolescents and adults even if they were vaccinated in childhood. Infants typically develop the most severe complications, including pneumonia and seizures. Dehydration and malnutrition are also common in infants and young children because the frequent coughing spells interfere with eating and drinking, and the vomiting that may follow coughing expels any water and food that might have been ingested. In adults, particularly those who were previously vaccinated against whooping cough, the only symptom of an infection may be a persistent cough.[4] Based on analysis of **antibodies** directed against *B. pertussis* **antigens**, as many as one-third of adults with a cough lasting longer than two weeks may have whooping cough.[5] (Antibodies are proteins, produced by **immune system** cells, in response to infection. Antigens are molecules, often proteins, that are bound by antibodies.)

Transmission of the disease is primarily through inhalation of airborne bacteria expelled from an infected person during coughing or sneezing. Whooping cough can also be acquired through direct contact with phlegm from the throat of an infected person. The attack rate for uninfected people living in the same house as a person with whooping cough is 80 percent or higher. Prior to the development of a vaccine, it was estimated that one case of whooping cough would lead to the infection of about 15 new victims. This makes whooping cough one of the most transmissible human diseases.

THE CAUSATIVE AGENT: *BORDETELLA PERTUSSIS*

The medical term for whooping cough is *pertussis*, from the Latin meaning "intense cough." This disease is caused by the bacterium *Bordetella pertussis*, a small microbe that requires oxygen to grow. The bacteria have a rounded rod shape. *B. pertussis* belongs to a large group of bacteria called **Gram negative** bacteria, which have an inner and outer membrane, separated by a thin cell wall, and stain pink when treated with a series of dyes (Gram staining). The organism is found only in the respiratory tract and can be found from the nasal passages down to the **bronchioles**. (Bronchioles are the smallest tubelike extensions of the air passages in the lungs.) *B. pertussis* normally does

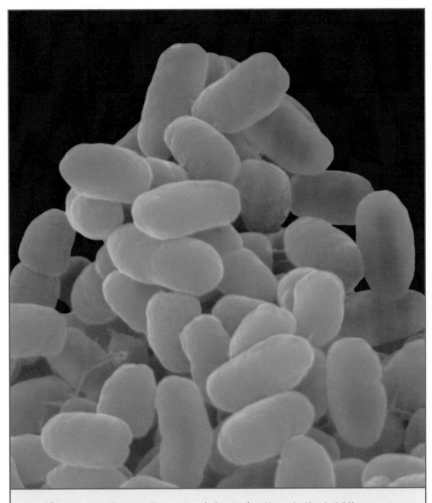

Figure 1.1 *Bordetella pertussis* **bacteria. (Dennis Kunkel Microscopy, Visuals Unlimited, Inc.)**

not get into the bloodstream, and does not infect other organs and tissues.

B. *pertussis* has been reported to cause disease only in humans; to date no animal hosts have been identified. In about 5 percent of cases, whooping cough has also been caused by related bacteria, including *Bordetella parapertussis*, although the symptoms tend to be milder than with disease caused by B. pertussis.[6] **DNA sequence** comparisons suggest that B. pertussis and B. parapertussis separately evolved from a genetically similar bacterium, Bordetella bronchiseptica. B. bronchiseptica is a pathogen that causes disease in a variety of animals, although it occasionally can infect humans. These animal and human pathogens have dramatically different lifestyles. B. bronchiseptica, can remain in the respiratory tract of an infected host, sometimes for the rest of the animal's life. In contrast, B. pertussis will normally be eliminated after one to two months. Theoretical considerations suggest that the widespread distribution of B. pertussis occurred once human populations in cities reached a high enough level that whooping cough could be maintained year-round, and from year-to-year. Under these conditions, a pathogen that causes intense, short-lived infections (as is the case with B. pertussis) is likely to be more successful than microbes that cause a milder, long-term infection.[7]

EPIDEMIOLOGY

Historically, outbreaks of whooping cough have peaked in three- to five-year cycles, most often in summer and early fall. These cycles are most likely the result of many children contracting whooping cough, leading to a sharp rise in the number of cases. Once these children recover, they become immune to re-infection, leading to a drop in the number of cases. By the third to fifth year, enough children lacking immunity would have been born that an epidemic could again spread through the population.

Whooping cough was rampant worldwide prior to the widespread deployment of vaccination in the 1940s, and almost everyone developed whooping cough during childhood. Even today, every year there are about 50 million cases and 300,000 deaths due to whooping cough across the globe. About 90 percent of these cases and deaths are in the developing world, particularly in countries with low vaccination rates.[9]

However, even in many developed countries, including the United States, the number of cases of whooping cough has

WHOOPING COUGH AND SLEEPWALKING

Sleep disorders often occur when a patient is partially aroused from sleep, becomes confused, and subsequently engages in some physical activity, like sleepwalking. A 2006 report from a hospital in Israel showed that sleepwalking might be a frequent side effect of whooping cough. In this group of patients, six of 60 (10 percent) sleepwalked during the night. The breathing difficulty associated with whooping cough caused these children to be partially awakened several times during the night; these awakenings were often followed by sleepwalking. Subsequent follow up showed that sleepwalking abated in all these patients when the symptoms of whooping cough diminished.[8]

increased steadily since the 1970s. For example, in 1976 there were 1,010 cases in the United States, and in 2006 there were more than 15,000 cases. It is likely, however, that these numbers represent a substantial underestimation of the true incidence of whooping cough, as many cases in adolescents and adults do not require medical treatment and are therefore unreported. Even so, about half the recently reported cases were in teenagers and adults.

It is not entirely clear what factors are responsible for the increasing incidence of whooping cough. One factor might simply be improved diagnosis due to better technology and more awareness of the disease in adolescents and adults. A more important factor is likely the waning immunity in people who were last vaccinated more than a decade ago. Consequently, in the United States, it is now recommended that teenagers get an additional whooping cough vaccination. There is also some evidence of the bacteria themselves changing. The use of the vaccine may be leading to the rise in strains of B. pertussis that are less affected by the immune response following vaccination.[10]

DISEASE AND DEATH

In the United States in the 1930s, the decade before the widespread use of the whooping cough vaccine, there were more than 200,000 cases of whooping cough per year, and nearly 8,000 deaths. In 2006 there were 15,600 cases of whooping cough and 27 deaths. This data represents a 92 percent reduc-

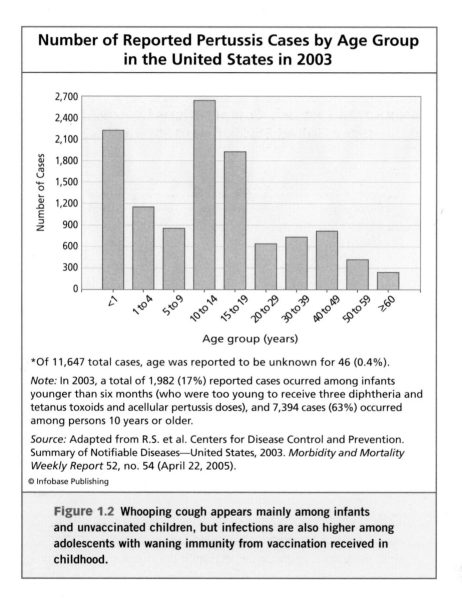

Number of Reported Pertussis Cases by Age Group in the United States in 2003

*Of 11,647 total cases, age was reported to be unknown for 46 (0.4%).

Note: In 2003, a total of 1,982 (17%) reported cases ocurred among infants younger than six months (who were too young to receive three diphtheria and tetanus toxoids and acellular pertussis doses), and 7,394 cases (63%) occurred among persons 10 years or older.

Source: Adapted from R.S. et al. Centers for Disease Control and Prevention. Summary of Notifiable Diseases—United States, 2003. *Morbidity and Mortality Weekly Report* 52, no. 54 (April 22, 2005).

© Infobase Publishing

Figure 1.2 Whooping cough appears mainly among infants and unvaccinated children, but infections are also higher among adolescents with waning immunity from vaccination received in childhood.

tion in cases, and a 99 percent reduction in deaths since the early decades of the twentieth century.[11]

Worldwide, the majority of whooping cough deaths reported in 2002 were in Africa and Southeast Asia, where fewer than 70 percent of children had received at least three doses of the vaccine. (In contrast, in the United States and most of Europe, more than 90 percent of children had received three or more doses of the vaccine by age six months. The recommended vaccine schedule for whooping cough is three doses of vaccine by six months of age.) In 2002 whooping cough

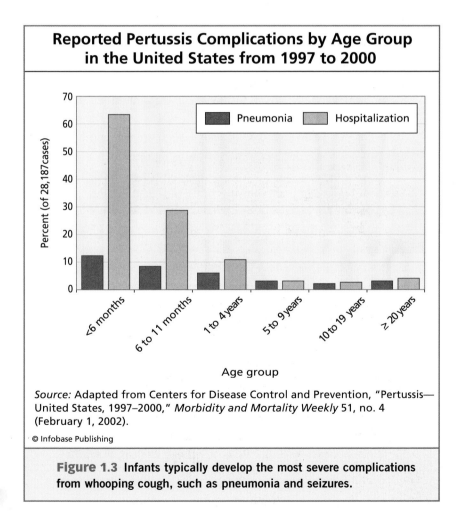

Reported Pertussis Complications by Age Group in the United States from 1997 to 2000

Source: Adapted from Centers for Disease Control and Prevention, "Pertussis—United States, 1997–2000," *Morbidity and Mortality Weekly* 51, no. 4 (February 1, 2002).

© Infobase Publishing

Figure 1.3 Infants typically develop the most severe complications from whooping cough, such as pneumonia and seizures.

MIGRAINE HEADACHES AND WHOOPING COUGH

In its advanced stages, symptoms of whooping cough are usually obvious and unambiguous. In some cases, however, people with whooping cough develop unusual symptoms. In a 2005 report a 10-year-old girl came into a headache clinic in Israel complaining of intense migraines. Her headaches occurred three to four times per week, and were often triggered or made worse by exposure to light. She had had these severe headaches for two months, which coincided with the length of her persistent cough. Her coughing episodes were often intense, and sometimes ended with the young girl vomiting. Blood tests showed that she had a current whooping cough infection. The doctors treated her with medicine for her headache and an antibiotic to kill *B. pertussis.* As her coughing diminished, her headaches became less intense. After six weeks she no longer had a cough, and her headaches had abated, indicating a link between whooping cough and her migraine headaches.

Her mother also had a history of migraines, spanning decades. These had improved with time, with relatively few headaches in the last few years. However, a few weeks before her daughter went into the clinic, the mother had developed more frequent headaches. She also developed a cough, and diagnostic testing indicated she had developed whooping cough. As with her daughter, as the mother's coughing diminished, so did the frequency of her headaches, further supporting the link between whooping cough and migraine headaches.[13]

Exactly how whooping cough might have led to migraines in these two cases is unclear. It is known that a lack of sleep can contribute to migraines, and whooping cough often interrupts sleep. In addition, whooping cough has been linked to other neurological conditions, such as seizure. It is therefore possible that these two individuals might have been particularly susceptible to components of *B. pertussis,* which led to their headaches.

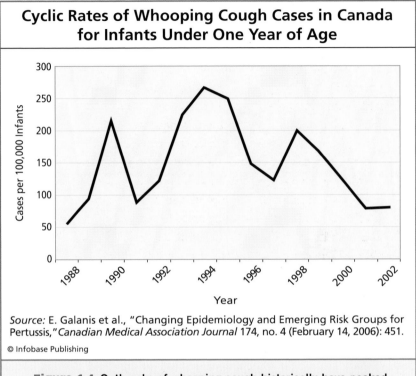

Cyclic Rates of Whooping Cough Cases in Canada for Infants Under One Year of Age

Source: E. Galanis et al., "Changing Epidemiology and Emerging Risk Groups for Pertussis," *Canadian Medical Association Journal* 174, no. 4 (February 14, 2006): 451.

© Infobase Publishing

Figure 1.4 Outbreaks of whooping cough historically have peaked in three- to five-year cycles, most often in summer and early fall. These cycles are most likely the result of many children contracting whooping cough, leading to a sharp rise in the number of cases. Once they recover, these children become immune to re-infection, leading to a drop in the number of cases.

accounted for 11 percent of the deaths from vaccine-preventable diseases in children under five years of age. In developing countries with low vaccination coverage, up to 4 percent of children who contract whooping cough die.[12]

2
The History of Whooping Cough

"Mrs. B., having a cough for two weeks, which was ascertained to be that of pertussis [whooping cough], came from Boston to a family in New York. She remained with the family from 2 P.M. . . . 'til the evening, when she left the city. During her stay she held and kissed an infant that was previously well and had never been removed from the floor on which it was born. . . . Four days after exposure, the infant began to cough, and this proved to be the beginning of a severe attack." This report, from 1892, showed that physicians were already aware that whooping cough was an infectious disease, almost 15 years before the isolation of the causative agent.[1] This report also shows how readily the disease can be transmitted from person to person.

Whooping cough has probably been an important human disease for thousands of years. Comparisons of the DNA sequences of *Bordetella pertussis* with other Bordetella species suggest that *B. pertussis* evolved from an animal pathogen hundreds of thousands of years ago. However, written descriptions of whooping cough are fairly recent, suggesting a relatively short history for *B. pertussis*, at least in Europe and the Middle East.[2] The first probable report of whooping cough came from Avicenna, a tenth century Middle Eastern physician. He described a childhood disease, characterized by violent coughing that caused the patient to become red-faced, and often resulted in spitting up blood. Subsequently, there were reports suggestive of whooping cough from the Netherlands, France, and other parts of Europe in the fourteenth and fifteenth centuries.[3] In 1578 the French physician Guillanne de Ballon gave a clear description of whooping cough:

> The lung is so irritated that in the efforts it makes to get rid of that which affects it, it can inhale and exhale only with difficulty. One would say that the patient swells up, and nearly suffocated, feels as though his breath was stopped in the middle of his throat. . . . The torment of the cough is sometimes suspended for four or five hours, after which a paroxysm returns which is often so violent that it causes blood to issue from the nose and mouth and very frequently it upsets the stomach and causes vomiting.[4]

Subsequently, there were many reports of whooping cough during the 1600s and 1700s from many places in Europe.[5] In 1679 English physician Thomas Sydenham first used the term *pertussis*, which means "violent cough."[6] The common names of whooping cough in a number of countries between 1500 and 1800 indicated a widespread awareness of the symptoms of the disease. For example, the disease was called *kink* (a fit) in Scotland, *wolfshusten* (howling of wolves) or *eselshusten* (braying of donkeys) in Germany, *tosse canina* (barking of dogs) in Italy, and *chincough* (boisterous laughter) in England.[7]

Subsequent accounts give a sense of the anxiety this disease must have caused for both infected children and their parents. For example, an 1892 textbook of infant diseases gives a description of whooping cough that provides insight into the distress that occurs during a coughing fit: [8]

> The severity of the cough in the second stage varies considerably in different cases. It sometimes commences quite abruptly, with little warning, but commonly there is premonition to it, and the child endeavors to repress it. He experiences a tickling sensation in the throat or median line of the chest, or a feeling of constriction. He

leaves his playthings and rests his head on his mother's lap or takes hold of some firm object for support; his face has a grave or even anxious appearance, while the pulse and respiration are somewhat accelerated. Immediately, the cough begins. It consists in a series of short and hurried expirations, which expel a large part of the air contained in the lungs, followed by a hurried inspiration. . . . The sound which accompanies the inspiration, and which is often absent, especially in infants, is designated the whoop. . . . The cough commonly ends in the expulsion of frothy mucus, and sometimes in vomiting. . . . the face is flushed and swollen and occasionally hemorrhage occurs under the conjunctiva [in the eyes] or from one of the mucus surfaces.

DISCOVERY OF THE CAUSATIVE AGENT

Early conjecture on the nature of the disease included some type of infectious agent. For example, in 1766 Swedish professor Nils Rosen von Rosenstein stated that "[t]he true cause of this disease [whooping cough] must be a heterogeneous matter or seed which has multiplicative power. . . . We find that it is communicated by infection and that a part of it is attracted by the breath down into the lungs."[9] However, early ideas about the cause of whooping cough did not always focus on a microbe. The nature of the disease suggested to some that the ailment was caused by a nervous system disorder, which produced a tickling in the throat. For example, in 1850 a physician in Philadelphia suggested that the cause of whooping cough was a malady of part of the brain.[10] (Recall that, in 1850, no bacterium had yet been identified as the cause of any disease.) A report from 1890 still described the cause as being the result of an unnamed "specific principle" that disturbs the nerves of the respiratory tract through the collection of mucus in the throat.[11]

By the late 1800s a number of microbiologists had reported identifying a bacterium as the cause of whooping cough. However

Figure 2.1 Belgian microbiologist Jules Bordet, who, with fellow microbiologist Octave Gengou, isolated and identified the *Bordetella pertussis* bacteria in 1906. (National Library of Medicine)

the identify of these potential pathogens could not be confirmed.[12] In 1901 the physician Marcus Hatfield stated, "it is generally conceded that a microorganism is the . . . cause of pertussis, but its natural history has not yet been definitely settled."[13]

Finally, in 1906, Belgian microbiologists Jules Bordet and Octave Gengou reported the isolation of *Bordetella pertussis*. Bordet and Gengou had developed a medium that included an extract from boiled potatoes, glycerol, and human or rabbit blood, which supported the growth of *Bordetella*, but inhibited the growth of other microbes frequently found in the mouth and throat. (A slightly modified version of this medium, containing sheep blood, is still used and is called Bordet-Gengou agar.)

Bordet and Gengou initially took respiratory secretions from a five-month-old infant who had whooping cough, and placed the material on their growth medium. Many small bacteria, now identified as *Bordetella pertussis*, grew on the plate. Subsequently, they placed plates containing this medium under the mouths of children who had whooping cough, during a coughing spell, and isolated the same pathogen from these other patients.[14] Bordet went on to win the Nobel Prize in Physiology or Medicine in 1919, primarily for his work on understanding the immune response.[15]

Following the isolation of *B. pertussis*, work began in earnest on the development of a vaccine. By 1914, six different whooping cough vaccines were licensed in the United States. However, because of the different ways that these pharmaceutical companies grew *B. pertussis*, the number of bacteria in the different vaccines varied, and the degree to which the microbes produced immune-stimulating molecules also varied. Consequently the vaccines differed substantially in their effectiveness.[16]

In 1924 and 1929, vaccines against whooping cough were tested during epidemics on the Faroe Islands, off the coast of Scotland. A Danish physician, Thorvald Madsen, developed a vaccine that contained dead *B. pertussis*. During the 1924 outbreak, people who were vaccinated developed whooping cough at the same rate as those who were not. However, the vaccine reduced the severity of the illness. In 1929 a modified version of the vaccine, consisting of *B. pertussis* grown on Bordet-Gengou agar and then heat-killed, produced a 20 percent reduction in the likelihood of developing whooping cough, compared to those who did not receive a vaccine.[17]

In 1933 Louis Saur, a physician in Chicago, reported on a whooping cough vaccine similar to that developed by Madsen that showed some effectiveness. This vaccine helped contribute to a definitive test of the association of *B. pertussis* with whooping cough in humans. Four children were used in this experiment. Two had been vaccinated and two were unvaccinated. Initially, *B. pertussis* was isolated from a child with whooping cough, and grown on agar plates in the laboratory. After a second period of growth on new agar plates, *B. pertussis* was scraped off half the plate and suspended in sterile salt water. This suspension was passed through a filter that trapped bacteria, but allowed viruses to pass through. About one-half of a milliliter of this filtered fluid was injected into the noses and spread on the throats of the four boys. None of the children developed any symptoms after almost three weeks, which indicated that whooping cough was not caused by a virus. The investigators then scraped off the bacteria from the remaining half of the agar plate, resuspended the bacteria in sterile salt water, and applied a diluted sample of this solution containing about 140 bacteria to the nostrils of each boy. The two vaccinated boys showed no symptoms; in contrast, the two unvaccinated boys developed severe cases of whooping cough. This showed that *B. pertussis* caused whooping cough, and that the vaccine, at least in this small sample, was effective. (Of course, conducting such an experiment today, in which young children were deliberately exposed to a serious pathogen, would be considered completely unethical.)[18]

In 1932 Pearl Kendrick and her colleague Grace Eldering, researchers at the Michigan Department of Health, started work on an improved whooping cough vaccine. In this case they grew the bacteria on Bordet-Gengou agar plates containing sheep blood, then treated the microbes with a mercury compound (thimerosal) to inactivate them. A vaccine based on this methodology was tested in 1934, and showed promise. However, a similar trial conducted two years later by James Doull did not show that the vaccine reduced the incidence of whooping cough. Analyzing the data from these two trials, Kendrick and her colleagues thought that one factor that might have contributed to a different result was the concentration of bacteria used in the two vaccines. Subsequently, they developed a technique to standardize the number of bacteria in a solution. They measured light transmission through a solution of bacteria, and compared that light transmission to the light penetration through a suspension of glass beads of known quantity.

This testing eventually led to a method for determining vaccine effectiveness in mice. A dose of approximately 100 *B. pertussis* bacteria was injected into the brains of mice. If a vaccine were protective, the mice would not die from the injection. On the other hand, if the vaccine were not effective, the mice would die. In addition, a mouse toxicity test was developed to assay the likelihood that a vaccine would cause reactions in humans. This test was based on whether mice lost weight following vaccination. Together, the "vaccine potency test" and "toxicity test" became required methods for verifying the usefulness of different lots of whooping cough vaccines, and led to greater standardization of these medicines.[19] Consequently, the whooping cough vaccine became generally recognized as an effective and critical childhood vaccine, and was used in the United States beginning in the mid-1940s.[20]

However, over time, there were reports of adverse effects attributed to the whole-cell whooping cough vaccine, and so research began on creating component vaccines, which use only part of the bacterial cell. As early as 1937 an American vaccine manufacturer received a patent on a whooping cough vaccine that contained only one component of the bacteria, the pertussis toxin. Subsequently, a number of other pharmaceutical companies developed whooping cough vaccines that only used some of the components of *B. pertussis*, particularly the pertussis

Figure 2.2 Grace Eldering (above), and Pearl Kendrick (below), were researchers at the Michigan Department of Health who developed the first successful whooping cough vaccine. (Grand Rapids Public Library, Grand Rapids, Michigan)

toxin. In 1981 Japan approved the use of a whooping cough vaccine that did not contain whole *B. pertussis* cells. However, none of these component vaccines became widely used in the United States until 1992, when an **acellular vaccine**, consisting of only certain molecules of *B. pertussis*, was approved by the United States Food and Drug Administration. Subsequently, in 2001, whole-cell whooping cough vaccines were eliminated from the U.S. market, and only acellular vaccines are currently available.[21]

EARLY TREATMENTS FOR WHOOPING COUGH

During the 1800s, there was very little physicians could do to treat whooping cough. Yet the severity of the coughing prompted physicians and parents to try almost anything to relieve the symptoms of the disease. As with many infectious diseases, there have been a number of remedies reported that are of questionable effectiveness, and many of which might actually be harmful.

One example was the use of bromoform, a close chemical relative to chloroform. Chloroform was one of the few anesthetics available during the 1800s, and bromoform had similar sedative properties that were thought to reduce the severity of coughing fits. In a report from 1892, a physician from Michigan described his use of bromoform as a treatment for pertussis. It was given to the patients in water, with one to three drops of the chemical administered up to four times per day. In an article describing this treatment, several patients were highlighted. One was the case of a seven-week-old boy who had developed whooping cough and died following bromoform treatment, not necessarily a ringing endorsement of the drug. The article describes the infant's symptoms and treatment: ". . . [He] had been coughing one week; paroxysm [coughing fits] frequent. Under treatment, after eight or nine days, the paroxysms became less frequent and severe, but his strength had gradually failed...[by the nineteenth day] the cough had nearly ceased and he appeared to be a little stronger. This condition lasted two days; then… death superven[ed] on the twenty-third day. Whisky was given during the whole period of treatment."[22] The use of whisky or bromoform to treat two-month-old babies with pertussis is, of course, no longer a standard medical practice. Alcohol is not used to treat any infectious disease at present. Bromoform is now considered a probable human carcinogen, is toxic, can cause loss of consciousness, and may damage the liver and kidneys.[23]

A physician, writing in 1890, describes the use of carboxylic acid (phenol) vapors to treat the severe cough. Current safety literature about phenol describes it as a toxic and corrosive chemical, which is very poisonous by inhalation and can cause chemical burns.[24] Other treatments described for whooping cough included cocaine, which was used in a 5 percent solution for repeated application to the throat. The burning of sulfur and cresoline (a toxic, potentially cancer-causing chemical)

TREATMENT TO PREVENT VOMITING IN WHOOPING COUGH

One of the many problems associated with whooping cough is vomiting following a coughing fit. In addition to the unpleasantness of this condition, it can also cause malnutrition and dehydration, particularly in infants and young children. A medical device was developed in the early twentieth century to try to prevent vomiting. It consisted of an elastic belt that snugly wrapped around the abdomen.[25] Apparently, this constriction was sufficient to reduce the ability of the abdominal muscles to expel material from the stomach. Medical reports of the time touted its effectiveness, although it is no longer used as a treatment for whooping cough.[26]

were also touted as treatments.[27] Other drugs used to treat whooping cough included morphine (a highly addictive compound that suppresses cough and relieves pain) and chloral hydrate (a potentially addictive prescription drug that induces sleep).[28] These treatments were generally ineffective, however. One physician, writing in 1911, wrote that "whether these remedies are administered internally or externally, no matter, they are, and remain, without effect." He also wrote that the use of inhalants (such as carboxylic acid or sulfur) "only tortures the children, [and] we accomplish nothing with these remedies, for the disease progresses uninfluenced."[29] Even today, treatment options for whooping cough are limited once the disease has progressed to the stage where it causes a spasmodic cough.

3

The Biology of Whooping Cough

My son was 17 years old and generally in very good health. He awoke one night with a fitful, wheezing cough. It continued the next day, and into the next week. His condition was not improving, so I took him to an urgent care clinic. They ran a number of tests, and prescribed azithromycin, an antibiotic commonly used to treat whooping cough. Eventually his cough abated, and he had a full recovery. He had completed all of his vaccinations, but had not gotten a whooping cough booster shot, which had been recently recommended for teenagers. Subsequently, our local paper reported an outbreak of 14 cases of whooping cough in our community.[1]

Like all human pathogens, Bordetella pertussis *is well adapted to life inside the body. It has the capability of surviving onslaughts of the immune system, has developed mechanisms for efficiently extracting nutrients from its perch in the throat, and has evolved strategies for efficient transmission from person to person. As a consequence, this pathogen has been a scourge of humans for thousands of years.*

STAGES OF DISEASE

Whooping cough has a characteristic progression in people who have never been vaccinated. In these individuals, the disease typically proceeds through the following four stages:

- Incubation—During this stage, the disease is asymptomatic. It typi-cally lasts for seven to 10 days. This first stage starts when *Bordetella pertussis* establishes a foothold on the cells lining the upper respiratory tract. At least two proteins on the surface of the bacteria, filamentous hemaglutinin (FHA) and pertussis toxin (PTx) appear to be critical for colonization. Once bacterial numbers reach a critical level, the next stage begins.

- Catharral—During this stage, the first signs of illness begin to develop, although they are generally mild and nonspecific. This stage lasts 2 to 7 days, and the symptoms typically include loss of appetite, mild cough, and a runny nose.

- Paroxysmal—During this stage, the bacterial **toxins** begin spreading through the body, causing widespread damage, and resulting in the classical presentation of whooping cough. Once the toxins enter cells, the damage is done and treatments can only provide supportive care. This stage lasts from a week to two months, and is characterized by intense coughing fits, often followed by vomiting.

- Convalescent—During this stage, the severity of the cough gradually begins to abate, the bacteria are eradicated, and the patient begins to recover. This stage can last for weeks or months and is characterized by a gradual improvement in symptoms.

TRANSMISSION OF WHOOPING COUGH

Patients are most **contagious** (capable of spreading disease) during the catarrhal stage and during the first two weeks after onset often before diagnosis of pertussis is made.[2] This is likely advantageous to the microbe, since whooping cough can be transmitted to more people during the incubation phase, when people are still generally feeling well, as compared to a later stage of the disease, when victims would be confined to bed due to serious symptoms.

Pathogens that are transmitted through the air typically cause the most contagious diseases. This transmission is enhanced with pathogens that cause violent coughing, which leads to the release of little aerosol packets containing infectious bacteria. Simply

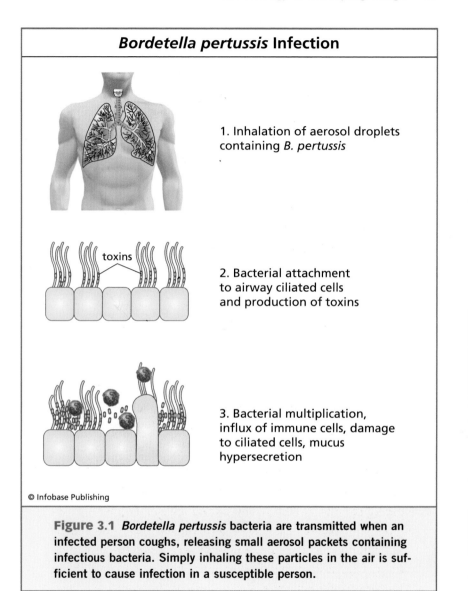

Bordetella pertussis Infection

1. Inhalation of aerosol droplets containing *B. pertussis*

toxins

2. Bacterial attachment to airway ciliated cells and production of toxins

3. Bacterial multiplication, influx of immune cells, damage to ciliated cells, mucus hypersecretion

© Infobase Publishing

Figure 3.1 *Bordetella pertussis* bacteria are transmitted when an infected person coughs, releasing small aerosol packets containing infectious bacteria. Simply inhaling these particles in the air is sufficient to cause infection in a susceptible person.

inhaling these particles in the air is sufficient to cause infection in a susceptible person. There is little information available on the dose of *B. pertussis* required to establish infection in humans. In one experiment, two unvaccinated children developed whooping cough when doctors inoculated about 140 bacteria into their nasal passages. (These children became very ill following their exposure to *B. pertussis*—they had coughing fits for more than a month. An experiment like that would not be permitted today.)[3] Further support that only a small dose of bacteria is required for infection comes from the observation that 75 to 100 percent of susceptible people develop the disease when exposed to an infected person.[4]

A DESCRIPTION OF WHOOPING COUGH TRANSMISSION

Even before it was understood what microbe caused whooping cough, it was clear that it was an infectious disease. As noted earlier, whooping cough is highly contagious. The following description, from a book published in 1909, is likely a little extreme in terms of the reported ease of transmission: [5]

> That pertussis is one of the most infectious diseases is well illustrated by the following history: On a bright cold day in December a patient of mine, nine months of age, passed in its carriage on the street a child about the same age who had pertussis. This child was also in its carriage. My patient took the disease. There was no other possible source of infection.

It is now known that people can transmit whooping cough without showing symptoms of the disease. Therefore, it is possible that the doctor's young patient acquired the disease from another person who may not have been showing signs of the disease, rather than from passing another child in a baby carriage. Modern biological laboratory techniques, not available at the time, could now test the hypothesis that the pathogen was transmitted by that brief interaction. This could be done, for example, through a detailed genetic comparison of the *B. pertussis* bacteria in the two children.

VIRULENCE FACTORS

The *B. pertussis* microbe has a number of weapons called **virulence factors** that allow it to survive and prosper in the human body. Among the most critical virulence factors are the toxins the microbe produces. One group of virulence factors includes **adhesins**, which are molecules that allow the bacteria to attach to human cells. Specifically, these molecules aid *B. pertussis* in attaching to the cells of the respiratory tract. **Fimbriae** are another virulence factor that consist of hairlike projections on the surface of the bacterial cell. They are also essential for the bacteria to stick to respiratory cells. Type IV **pili** (small stubby projections on the surface of bacterial cells) and peractin are other virulence factors involved in adherence.

Tracheal colonization factor is a surface protein genetically similar to peractin. Research in mice has shown that tracheal colonization factor is required for establishing an infection. Another critical virulence factor is called BrkA; this protein prevents *B. pertussis* from being destroyed by **complement**, an antibacterial component of the blood. A related molecule is PagP, a protein that modifies the outside of *B. pertussis* cells, and thereby helps hide the microbe from the immune system.

One of the key limitations on bacterial growth in the body is an absence of readily available iron. Although iron is fairly abundant inside the body (for example, it is a key component of oxygen-carrying **hemoglobin**) the iron is locked up so tightly that it is not easy for microbes in the body to access it. The bacterium that causes Lyme disease, *Borrelia burgdorferi*, gets around this problem by not needing iron—its proteins use other metals found in the body instead. Most bacteria, though, have special mechanisms for harvesting iron from human cells and proteins. Researchers believe that, because of the importance of iron for bacterial growth, *B. pertussis* uses multiple systems to extract iron from host cells and tissues. *B. pertussis* produces a small molecule called alcaligin A, which helps the bacteria grab iron from human cells and tissues.[6] In addition to alcaligin A, a group of *bhu* (Bordetella **h**eme **u**tilization) genes produce a surface protein that can

Table 3.1 Bacterial components important to the ability of Bordetella to cause disease

Bacterial component	Expressed by	Function	Comment	Acellular vaccine component
Filmaentous hemagglutinin	BP, BPa, BB	Adhesin (mediates adherence of bacteria to host structures)	Immunosuppressive activity may reduce life span of immunity	Yes
Pertactin	BP, BPa, BB	Adhesin		Yes
Fimbriae	BP, BPa, BB	Adhesin	Several different fimbrial types expressed by the different species	Yes: types 2 & 3
Pertussis toxin	BP	Catalyzes ADP ribosylation of host G-proteins, which causes a number of effects	Genes present in BPa and BB but not expressed; precise role in disease is unclear	Yes: inactivated toxin
Adenylate cyclase	BP, BPa, BB	Cytotoxin; synthesizes cAMP (cyclic adenosine monophos-phate) in host cells, which distrupts host cell physiology; anti-inflammatory effect through action on host immune cells		No
Type III secretion system	BB, BPa$_{ov}$	Alters host immune cell function; important for chronic infection	Genes present in BP and BPa$_{hu}$ but expression has not been detected in these species	No

			Role in virulence is unclear	No
Dermonecrotic toxin	BP, BPa, BB	Toxin; activates host GTP binding protein Rho; causes changes in host cell morphology		No
Tracheal colonization factor	BP	Adhesin?		No
BrkAB system	BP, some BB	Resistance to serum-mediated killing		No
Lipopolysaccharide	BP, BPa, BB	Structural component of bacterial outer membrane; proinflammatory activity; resistance to host defence molecules	Complex glycolipid; structure varies between species	No
Tracheal cytotoxin	BP, BPa, BB	Cytotoxin; contributes to damage to the respiratory epithelium	Cell wall breakdown product	No
BvgAS system	BP, BPa, BB	Global regulator of expression of most Bordetella virulence factors		No

Note: BP= *B. pertussis*, BPa= *B. parapertussis*, BPa$_{ov}$ =ovine-adapted *B. parapertussis*, BPa$_{hu}$ =human-adapted *B. parapertussis*, BB= *B. bronchiseptica*

Source: Andrew Preston, "*Bordetella pertussis*: The Intersection of Genomics and Pathobiology," *Canadian Medical Association Journal* 173, no. 1 (July 5, 2005): 57.

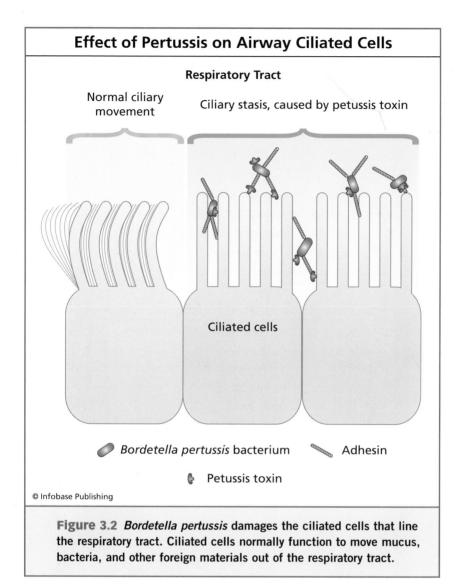

Effect of Pertussis on Airway Ciliated Cells

Respiratory Tract

Normal ciliary movement

Ciliary stasis, caused by petussis toxin

Ciliated cells

Bordetella pertussis bacterium   Adhesin

Petussis toxin

© Infobase Publishing

Figure 3.2 *Bordetella pertussis* **damages the ciliated cells that line the respiratory tract. Ciliated cells normally function to move mucus, bacteria, and other foreign materials out of the respiratory tract.**

directly bind to hemoglobin and related compounds, and bring these iron-containing molecules into the bacterial cell.[7]

Another virulence mechanism is evasion of the immune system. *B. pertussis* produces a molecular syringe called a **Type III secretion system**. This system injects proteins into eukaryotic cells, and helps inactivate immune system cells. Some of the *B.*

pertussis toxins make their way into human cells via this Type III secretion system. Other virulence factors include **flagella**, the long appendages that allow the bacteria to move, and a **capsule** surrounding the cell, made of sugars, which inhibits immune system cells from ingesting and destroying the microbes.

IMMUNE RESPONSE TO THE PATHOGEN

Whooping cough is most serious in infants because they have an undeveloped immune system. In contrast, older children and adults who have a fully functional immune system rarely suffer serious complications from infection with *B. pertussis*. This indicates that the appropriate immune response is critical to protection from disease.

For a number of diseases (for example, smallpox), a single exposure to the pathogen confers life-long immunity. Whooping cough is not one of those diseases. Whether exposed to *B. pertussis* through vaccination or actual infection, the protection conferred is relatively short-lived—usually a decade or two at most.[8]

The immune response can be divided into two separate yet complementary arms. One branch of the immune system, called the **innate immune response,** consists of molecules and cells that are constantly produced and are immediately ready to deal with an infection. The other branch of the immune response is the **adaptive immune response**, which consists of molecules and cells that specifically target a particular pathogen, but which takes a week or more to develop.

Following infection, the innate immune response triggers **neutrophils** and other white blood cells to find and attack the invading microbes. Initially this response may partially check *B. pertussis* growth. As the bacteria multiply and disease symptoms begin to appear, other components of the immune system come into play. Starting about seven days after infection, an adaptive immune response begins to develop. This consists of both an antibody response and a cellular response.

Antibodies are proteins produced by a type of white blood cell called a B cell. B cells are stimulated by exposure to antigens

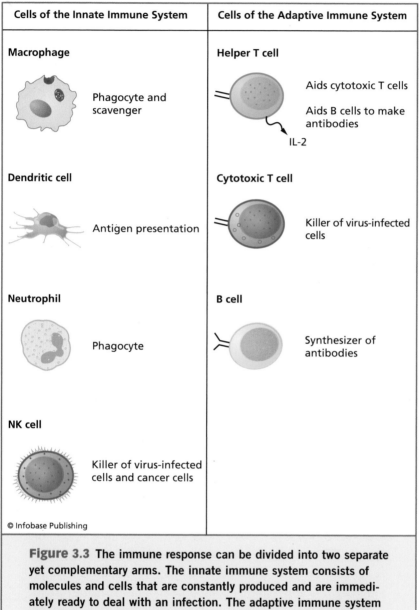

Cells of the Innate Immune System	Cells of the Adaptive Immune System
Macrophage Phagocyte and scavenger	**Helper T cell** Aids cytotoxic T cells Aids B cells to make antibodies IL-2
Dendritic cell Antigen presentation	**Cytotoxic T cell** Killer of virus-infected cells
Neutrophil Phagocyte	**B cell** Synthesizer of antibodies
NK cell Killer of virus-infected cells and cancer cells	

© Infobase Publishing

Figure 3.3 The immune response can be divided into two separate yet complementary arms. The innate immune system consists of molecules and cells that are constantly produced and are immediately ready to deal with an infection. The adaptive immune system consists of molecules and cells that specifically target a particular pathogen.

from a pathogen, which are typically displayed by antigen-presenting cells, including **macrophages**. Once stimulated, B cells begin to grow and divide and produce antibodies that specifically bind to that pathogen. Once attached, the antibodies act as a handle for other immune system cells, such as neutrophils or macrophages, to engulf and ingest the bacterial invaders. Antibodies also act as a catalyst for activating components in the blood, called complement, which can directly destroy microbes. Antibodies that are targeted against proteins on the surface of bacterial cells can prevent B. pertussis from binding to cells in the respiratory tract. In addition, antibodies can bind to and inactivate circulating toxins, thereby protecting cells.

Different types of antibodies are produced following infection. One type, called immunoglobulin M (IgM), is produced early in infection. IgG, produced subsequently, is primarily found in the bloodstream. IgA is produced primarily in the mucus membranes. This type of antibody is induced more by actual infection than vaccination, and appears to be highly effective in protection against whooping cough. Consequently, efforts are being made to develop vaccines that more strongly enhance IgA production in order to more effectively prevent whooping cough.[9]

During infection or following vaccination, antibodies are produced for a variety of bacterial components, including pertussis toxin, filamentous hemaglutinin, fimbrae, and peractin. Although antibodies to each individual component provided some protection, antibodies to a combination of these molecules provided stronger protection. This observation is being taken into account in the development of acellular whooping cough vaccines, which include only specific molecules, like pertussis toxin, filamentous hemaglutinin, and others. These vaccines typically contain multiple components, rather than a single antigen.[10]

B. pertussis has the ability to enter and survive in some types of human cells, including cells of the immune system,

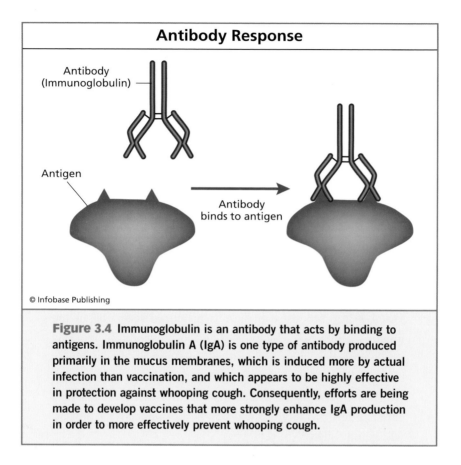

Antibody Response

Antibody
(Immunoglobulin)

Antigen

Antibody
binds to antigen

© Infobase Publishing

Figure 3.4 Immunoglobulin is an antibody that acts by binding to antigens. Immunoglobulin A (IgA) is one type of antibody produced primarily in the mucus membranes, which is induced more by actual infection than vaccination, and which appears to be highly effective in protection against whooping cough. Consequently, efforts are being made to develop vaccines that more strongly enhance IgA production in order to more effectively prevent whooping cough.

such as macrophages. Therefore a **cellular immune response**, which can home in on and destroy these intracellular bacteria, also appears to be important in ultimately controlling *B. pertussis* infection. (Interestingly, this response appears to be minimized in the acellular whooping cough vaccines, as compared with whole-cell vaccines.)[11]

In a cellular immune response, first, a type of white blood cell, called a **CD4+ T cell**, recognizes the foreign invader, in this case, the agent of whooping cough. This recognition activates the T cell, and causes it to produce chemicals and other signals that, in turn, activate other immune system cells. The CD4+ T cells activate macrophages that contain the intracellular bacteria, so that these infected cells can destroy the bacterial

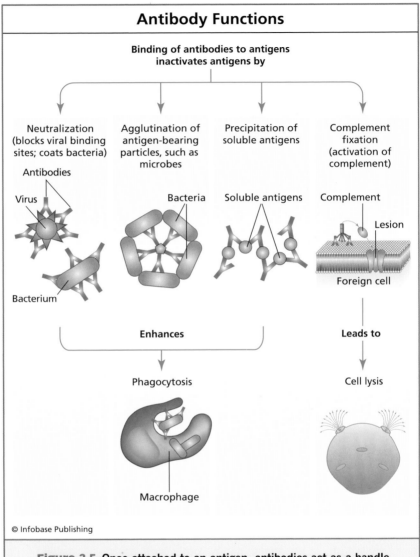

Figure 3.5 Once attached to an antigen, antibodies act as a handle for other immune system cells, such as neutrophils or macrophages, to engulf and ingest the bacterial invaders. Antibodies also act as a catalyst for activating components in the blood, called complement, which can directly destroy microbes. Antibodies that are targeted against proteins on the surface of bacterial cells can prevent *B. pertussis* from binding to cells in the respiratory tract. In addition, antibodies can bind to and inactivate circulating toxins, thereby protecting cells.

invaders. In addition, the CD4+ T cells activate the **cytotoxic T cells**, which are another type of immune system cell that specifically seeks out and destroys infected cells and the bacteria they contain.

BORDETELLA PERTUSSIS: AVOIDANCE OF THE IMMUNE RESPONSE

The fact that *B. pertussis* is a successful pathogen means that it has evolved ways of skirting the body's powerful immune responses. Many of these immune evasion mechanisms involve the production of toxins, which is described in detail in the next chapter. Here, however, is an overview of the microbes' counterattacks on the immune system, including the effect of the toxins.

When bacteria initially enter the body, they first encounter roving, bacteria-gobbling cells, including macrophages and neutrophils. If all goes well, these cells ingest and destroy the bacteria, and no infection develops. Unfortunately, in many cases, the bacteria are able to fend off this initial attack by the immune system. For example, *B. pertussis* produces adenylate cyclase toxin, which, once it enters macrophages, prevents those cells from killing ingested bacteria. This same toxin also inhibits neutrophils from ingesting *B. pertussis*.[12] In addition, pertussis toxin reduces the infiltration of macrophages and neutrophils to the site of *B. pertussis* infection. Tracheal toxin also inhibits migration of neutrophils to the site of infection, and reduces the ability of the cells that contact *B. pertussis* to kill the microbe.[13]

Another potentially harmful effect of various components of *B. pertussis* is interference with communication between cells. In the absence of *B. pertussis*, immune system cells like macrophages and **dendritic cells** send chemical signals and physically process parts of ingested microbes, presenting them on their surfaces in order to activate other key immune system cells. Adenylate cyclase toxin, along with the bacterial compo-

IMMUNE AVOIDANCE IN OTHER BORDETELLA SPECIES

Antibodies are often a key mechanism for keeping pathogens at bay. *Bordetella pertussis* has mechanisms for avoiding the damaging effects of antibodies. Analysis of a closely related species, *B. bronchiseptica,* indicates that it has another mechanism for evading the host immune response. Researchers from the University of California–Santa Barbara reported on the identification of a *B. bronchiseptica* protein that binds antibodies in mice. This appears to play a critical role in the survival of this pathogen in mammals. When the protein is eliminated by a genetic mutation, the bacteria are not able to survive in the lungs long-term. In contrast, strains of *B. bronchiseptica* that contain this protein are able to survive for an extended period in the lungs of mice.

A gene encoding the same protein is found in *B. pertussis,* but the protein is apparently not expressed in this microbe. *B. bronchiseptica* can infect a wide range of mammals, and *B. pertussis* only infects humans. Differences in the genes expressed by each organism, such as this antibody-binding protein, likely help explain this difference in host range.[14]

nents filamentous hemaglutinin and peractin, exert suppressive effects on **phagocytic cells**.[15] As a consequence, these cells do not send out the appropriate chemical signals, and do not present antigens, so a more adaptive immune response is delayed.

Another key element of the immune response is complement. Complement can aid in the ingestion of pathogens by immune system cells, and it can also directly kill some microbes by creating a hole in the bacterial cell membrane. Complement exists as a group of inactive proteins in the bloodstream. In the presence of some bacterial surface structures, one pathway of complement activation can occur, called the alternate complement pathway. *B. pertussis* lacks these surface structures, so it does not activate complement through this pathway. The other pathway of complement activation occurs after antibodies bind to the surface of bacterial cell. Once an antibody binds, the portion of the molecule protruding away from the surface of the bacteria can activate complement. *B. pertussis* produces a protein, BrkA (Bordetella resistance to killing), which prevents complement from forming a complex that creates a hole in the bacterial membrane, thereby blunting this immune response.[16]

B. pertussis has clearly evolved a number of mechanisms to avoid immune responses that protect us against other pathogens. This evasion of normal host response to infection contributes to the success of *B. pertussis* as a human pathogen.

ANIMAL MODELS FOR THE STUDY OF WHOOPING COUGH

Animal models are critical for understanding disease processes and developing improved treatments and vaccines, in part because it is easier to study the effects of vaccination and immunity within a population of animals than among humans. *B. pertussis* is a uniquely human pathogen, so one of the challenges with animal models for this disease is to establish whooping cough infections in unnatural hosts.

Mice have been the most commonly used models for studying whooping cough. For example, mice have been used as early as the 1940s to test the potency of vaccines and the likelihood of vaccine side effects. The original mouse model involved injecting *B. pertussis* into the brains of mice. More recent protocols have infected mice by placing the bacteria in the nose or by aerosolizing the bacteria and allowing the mice to inhale the microbes. These infected mice show some symptoms of human disease (e.g., weight loss) but not others, such as coughing, since mice cannot cough.

GENETIC REGULATION OF VIRULENCE

Bacterial cells use energy when they make proteins and other molecules. Virulence factors are typically proteins, and they are normally only required when the bacteria are inside a human host. Consequently, to avoid wasting energy, almost all pathogens regulate their production of virulence factors, and *B. pertussis* is no exception.

In the case of *B. pertussis*, the primary regulation occurs through the action of a group of genes called the bvg (**B**ordetella **v**irulence **g**enes) locus. There are two primary components to this regulatory system. One component, *bvgS*, is a gene that encodes the BvgS protein. This protein is embedded in the cell membrane and senses environmental signals. The nature of the

Whooping cough has also been modeled using newborn piglets. When infected with *B. pertussis* between the ages of one to four weeks, these animals show more symptoms of whooping cough compared to mice, including runny noses and coughs. Compared to mice, it is also easier to study immune responses in piglets. Piglets, however, do not exhibit the intense coughing fits that are characteristic of human whooping cough. Rats do develop an intense cough following infection with *B. pertussis*. However, they do not develop a runny nose or other symptoms of human disease. Under experimental conditions, nonhuman primates have been infected with *B. pertussis* and have developed typical whooping cough and have transmitted the disease to other animals. Primates are expensive to work with, however, and the ethical issues surrounding experimentation with these animals limit their use.

The availability of several animal models, particularly mice and newborn piglets, should provide a better understanding of whooping cough, and the ability to test new vaccines for safety and efficacy.[17]

signals detected by this protein is not entirely clear, but one of the signals detected is temperature. At 37°C (98.6°F), the BvgS protein detects that it is in the body and becomes activated. As a result, it gains a phosphate group. This phosphate is then attached to the BvgA protein, which is a transcriptional regulator. BvgA then binds to different regions of DNA and either activates or represses transcription of different genes.

One analysis, by researchers at Stanford University and UCLA, showed that the BvgA protein activates 288 genes and turns down the expression of 250 genes. The activated genes include a wide range of virulence factors, such as pertussis, adenylate cyclase, and other toxins, as well as Type III secretion systems, adhesions, fimbrae, and filamentous hemaglutinin.[18]

Perhaps equally important for the survival of B. pertussis, is that if BvgS is not getting a signal that it is inside the body, it shuts off these virulence genes. In addition, a relatively small group of genes are expressed when BvgS is not active, and these genes appear to aid cell survival when nutrients are limited, as would be the case outside the body. These genes include those involved in making the cell envelope, the genes involved in energy metabolism, and the genes involved in protein folding.[19] It appears that these two genes, bvgA and bvgS, have the potential to control a wide array of other genes that are critical for establishing infection.

Another aspect of virulence regulation is the production of biofilms. Biofilms describe bacteria that are embedded in a matrix, and the biofilm typically protects the microbe from damage from environmental factors. For example, B. pertussis growing in a biofilm was shown to be 160 to 1,000 times more resistant to antibiotics used to treat whooping cough, versus the same organism growing outside a biofilm. Biofilm production is also regulated by the Bvg gene, and it is likely that a biofilm is produced inside the body during an infection. This could consequently complicate efforts to treat B. pertussis infections with antibiotics or other methods.[20]

Another example of virulence gene regulation in *B. pertussis* involves proteins that aid the cell in taking up iron from the human host. One cluster of genes (the *bhu* genes) is specialized for extracting iron from heme, an iron-containing key component of the oxygen-carrying hemoglobin in the blood. Since it costs energy for the cell to make proteins, *B. pertussis* makes the Bhu proteins only when it is lacking iron yet has access to heme. The mechanism behind this regulation involves at least three proteins: Fur, which blocks transcription of HurI and HurR if iron is present; and HurR, which binds to HurI and prevents HurI from functioning if heme is absent. If iron is absent inside the cell, and heme is present in the environment, HurI is active, and allows the transcription of the *bhu* genes, resulting in heme uptake.[21]

4

The Toxins of
Bordetella pertussis

Bacterial toxins are biological poisons that play an important role in many infectious diseases, including whooping cough. These toxins often have a highly specific function that allows them to target particular tissues in a way that favors the growth of the bacteria. These toxins are exquisitely tuned to interact with and alter critical cell functions. In many cases, an understanding of how these toxins function has come from studies of bacterial mutants that lack a functional toxin gene or genes. This chapter presents an overview of the key toxins of *Bordetella pertussis,* and how they contribute to whooping cough.

GENERAL CHARACTERISTICS OF BACTERIAL TOXINS

Toxins are critical virulence factors for many pathogens. Many toxins are highly specific in their action, often affecting just a single protein (for example, the adenylate cyclase toxin from *B. pertussis*). Other toxins affect a wide range of host cells (for example, **hemolysins** produced by *Staphylococcus aureus*). Several bacterial toxins are among the most potent poisons known. For example, an amount of botulism toxin equivalent to about 1/60th of a small grain of sand (165 ng) is enough to kill a 150 lb (68 kg) person.[1]

Toxins can be classified in a variety of ways. For example, some toxins are secreted from the bacterial cell—these are called **exotoxins**. Exotoxins are normally proteins. Toxins that remain either inside or attached to the outside of bacterial cells are called **endotoxins**. Endotoxins include lipopolysaccharides, a component of the cell envelope in Gram-negative bacteria.

Toxins are also characterized by their structure. For example, many toxins, like pertussis toxin, are called A-B toxins. These toxins possess an active section (the A domain), which typically gets inside the host cell and alters some key function. The other portion of the toxin (the B domain) is involved in binding the toxin to the host cell, and internalizing the toxin. The RTX toxins, which includes adenylate cyclase toxin from *B. pertussis,* are another important group. These toxins contain a region that acts as a pore for entry of the toxin into the cell.

In general, for pathogens that produce toxins, many of the symptoms of the diseases they cause can be directly linked to the toxin. The specific toxins produced by *B. pertussis*, and the characteristics and effects of those toxins are described below.

PERTUSSIS TOXIN

The key toxin associated with whooping cough is pertussis toxin. This toxin plays several roles during infection, including adhesion to respiratory tract cells, and blunting the immune response.

As noted previously, pertussis toxin is an A-B toxin, which is a type of exotoxin. In the case of the pertussis toxin, the B domain consists of five subunits. These subunits allow the toxin to bind to a molecule on the surface of human cells. Once attached to the cell surface, the entire toxin is brought into the cell, where the active domain is released.

The active domain then interacts with a human protein called **calmodulin**, which makes the toxin functional. Pertussis toxin then inactivates regulatory proteins inside human cells called **G proteins,** by attaching a chemical group to them. These G proteins have diverse roles inside the cell, so the effects of their disruption cause a variety of symptoms, including low blood sugar as a result of high insulin production, sensitivity to histamine (an immune system molecule that contributes to symptoms of allergy), and the presence of large numbers of white blood cells in the circulation. In terms of aiding the bacteria in establishing infection, pertussis toxin appears to inhibit the ability of white blood cells to leave the bloodstream and enter a site of infection, such as places where *B. pertussis* is replicating. In addition, the toxin reduces the response of white blood cells that reach a site of infection, thus reducing the likelihood they will kill *B. pertussis*.

In spite of a prevailing wisdom that pertussis toxin is central to the symptoms of whooping cough, that fact is not yet

PROTEIN SECRETION IN BACTERIA

Bacteria have many ways of secreting proteins outside the cell. In particular, Gram-negative bacteria, like *Bordetella pertussis*, make use of groups of proteins, called secretion systems, to efficiently move proteins outside the cell. These systems have mechanisms to get the protein across the inner membrane, the cell wall, and the outer membrane of the bacterial cells. Some secretion systems also include a mechanism for injecting virulence proteins into human cells.

- Type I secretion systems consist of a pore that extends from the inner membrane through the outer membrane. These systems can transport proteins and other molecules, and are responsible for the translocation of a variety of bacterial toxins.

- Type II secretion systems use a general pathway to get proteins across the inner membrane and a specialized protein complex in the outer membrane.

- Type III secretion systems are analogous to bacterial flagella and act like a tiny syringe to inject proteins into a human cell. Type III secretion systems have been identified in a wide range of bacterial pathogens.

entirely clear. Perhaps the most penetrating analysis of the role of pertussis toxin comes from the study of another microbe, *B. parapertussis*, which produces similar symptoms to *B. pertussis*, but does not produce pertussis toxin. A comparison of disease symptoms from people infected with the two different organisms suggests that pertussis toxin is particularly associated with higher levels of white blood cells in the bloodstream and an

- Type IV secretion systems are apparently derived from proteins that are involved in the transfer of genetic information between bacteria. These systems can transfer DNA or proteins (or both), frequently directly into another cell.

- Type V secretion systems use the general secretion pathway to transport proteins across the inner bacterial membrane. Then the protein itself forms a pore to enable the transport of the remainder of the protein across the outer membrane. In some cases the protein is cleaved, releasing a portion of the protein into the environment. This system is sometimes called the autotransporter pathway.

- Type VI secretion systems do not use the general secretion pathway. They were first named in 2006 and differ from other secretion systems in the types of proteins that are used for transport across the membranes.

Functional Type III, IV, and V secretion systems have been identified in *B. pertussis*, and additional transporters are likely to be uncovered as research on the genetics of this organism continues. Since these transporters appear to play a critical role in pathogenesis, a better understanding of these transporters may lead to new treatments for a variety of bacterial diseases, including whooping cough.[2]

overall greater severity of disease symptoms and an increased risk of death. However, there does not appear to be an association between the toxin and severe coughing fits.[3]

In recent years, a clearer understanding has emerged of how pertussis toxin exits *B. pertussis* cells. The toxin is exported to the **periplasm** (the space between the inner and outer membrane of *B. pertussis*). The *ptl* gene encodes a pertussis toxin transporter,

USES OF THE *BORDETELLA PERTUSSIS* TOXINS IN RESEARCH

Bacterial toxins have been studied extensively in biological research to better understand cell physiology and metabolism. Bacterial toxins have also been used as a way of reporting on certain activities within a cell. This latter situation is the basis for several uses of adenylate cyclase toxin from *B. pertussis* in biological research.

In one example, researchers attached the active portion of the adenylate cyclase protein to a bacterial protein they suspected was injected into human cells. When they mixed the bacteria and human cells together, they were able to detect high levels of adenylate cyclase activity inside the human cells. This indicated that the other bacterial protein had been injected into the human cells.

A modification of this system was also used as a way to screen for new drugs to fight human immunodeficiency virus (HIV). In this case, two sections of the adenylate cyclase protein were joined together with a section of an HIV protein in between them. In that configuration, the adenylate cyclase worked, and would produce cyclic AMP, which could be readily detected.

In HIV infections, the virus produces an enzyme that cleaves the section of the HIV protein that is included in this model system. Therefore, a system is set up with the HIV-joined adenylate cyclase enzyme and a regulated copy of the which is embedded in the outer membrane. The Ptl protein is a Type IV secretion system that moves the toxin across the final cellular barrier, the outer membrane.[4] It appears that the bacteria require a specific chemical from the host, **reduced glutathione**, in order to efficiently excrete the toxin. This chemical is present at high concentrations in the respiratory tract in humans, which is the site of infection for *B. pertussis*. Consequently, this microbe

HIV protease (an enzyme that cuts up other proteins). So if the protease is active, there will not be any adenylate cyclase activity. However, if a drug that inhibits the protease is present in the solution, it will not cleave the protein, and the adenylate cyclase activity will be preserved.[5]

Another potential use of adenylate cyclase is in the development of better vaccines. One goal is to develop vaccines that more effectively induce a cellular immune response, as this is critical in protection against some diseases, including tuberculosis.

In work reported in 2002, researchers from the Czech Republic and France constructed a model vaccine by first genetically inactivating the adenylate cyclase gene, and then attaching a sequence from an unrelated protein that was known to be active in cellular immune response. Initially tests were done in isolated mouse cells, which showed that the cells were able to take up the combined protein and display appropriate portions to T cells. Further work was then done in live mice, which were injected with the most effective combinations, based on the in vitro tests. These mice developed an appropriate immune response, suggesting that adenylate cyclase from *B. pertussis* might have use in future vaccine development for illnesses that require a cellular immune response.[6]

takes advantage of products produced in abundance by its host to establish infection and cause disease.[7]

ADENYLATE CYCLASE TOXIN

The adenylate cyclase toxin is produced as a single protein inside the bacterial cell and is similar to toxins produced by a variety of bacterial pathogens. Following modification by another protein, the adenylate cyclase toxin is secreted to the outside of the cell. In most cases, the toxin remains associated to the bacterial cell until it binds to a specific molecule (CD11b) on human cells. At this point, the toxin gets moved inside the human cell, where it becomes activated through an interaction with a human protein, calmodulin. Once activated, this toxin cranks out large amounts of cyclic AMP, which regulates many cellular processes. In whooping cough, this toxin primarily affects immune system cells like neutrophils. The action of adenylate cyclase in these cells inhibits their ability to find, internalize, and destroy *B. pertussis*. The importance of this toxin in the disease process was clarified by studying bacterial mutants that did not produce the toxin, as well as mouse mutants that lacked certain aspects of a normal immune response. For example, *B. pertussis* strains lacking the toxin were unable to cause lethal infections in newborn mice, whereas normal *B. pertussis* strains effectively killed newborn mice. Similarly, in mice strains that had neutrophils but lacked T and B cells, *B. pertussis* strains lacking adenylate cyclase did not cause lethal infections, but in mice that lacked neutrophils and related cells, *B. pertussis* strains that lacked adenylate cyclase still caused lethal infections. This suggests that this toxin helps protect the bacteria from innate immune system cells like neutrophils.[8]

TRACHEAL TOXIN

As the name suggests, tracheal toxin damages cells in the upper respiratory tract. This toxin consists of fragments of the bacterial cell wall. In most bacteria, these cell wall fragments are recycled, but in *B. pertussis*, some of these fragments diffuse away from the cell wall. Once these cell wall fragments interact with human cells, they lead to the production of chemicals that damage the ciliated cells lining the respiratory tract. These ciliated cells normally function to move mucus, bacteria, and other foreign material out of the respiratory tract. The loss of these cells contributes to the ability of *B. pertussis* to persist in the respiratory tract, most likely contributes to coughing to help clear the respiratory tract, and increases the likelihood of secondary infections such as bacterial pneumonia.

OTHER TOXINS

B. pertussis produces other toxins that may play a role in the symptoms of whooping cough. For example, dermonecrotic toxin has been shown to cause localized tissue death and major changes in the cytoskeleton of cells. Its role in causing whooping cough has yet to be clearly established. In addition, *B. pertussis* is decorated with molecules called lipopolysaccharide. Lipopolysaccharides are endotoxins (bacterial-bound toxins) and are characteristic of Gram-negative bacteria. Lipopolysaccharides impair some host immune responses, and provide protection against certain host molecules, like complement, which otherwise might destroy the microbe.[9]

5

Diagnosis and Treatment of Whooping Cough

"Pure air is an essential part of the treatment of whooping cough. When the season is such as will permit, the child should be kept in the open air the larger part of the day. When the weather is inclement two rooms should be devoted to your patient in order that one room may be aired and warmed while the child is kept in the other and as often as feasible carried from one to the other."[1] Fortunately, medical treatments have advanced dramatically since 1901, when this passage was written. However, the diagnosis and treatment of whooping cough are still problematic in some ways.

DIAGNOSIS OF WHOOPING COUGH

A presumptive clinical diagnosis of whooping cough is based on the presence of a cough of at least two weeks duration, with either fits of coughing, a "whoop" sound, or vomiting after coughing, as determined by a health professional.[2]

A definitive diagnosis relies on identifying *Bordetella pertussis* in samples collected from the respiratory tract. The traditional method of identifying *B. pertussis* involves growing the microbe on appropriate culture medium in the laboratory. Collection of suitable samples for culturing *B. pertussis* can be challenging. Throat swabs are generally unsuitable for growing the microbe in culture, since many other bacteria are present and often overgrow the slow-growing *B. pertussis*. Either nasopharyngeal swabs or nasopharyngeal aspirates work best for sampling. Nasopharyngeal swabbing is performed by placing a small swab in one nostril and inserting it until it reaches the back of the throat. The swab is then twisted

Nasopharyngeal Swab

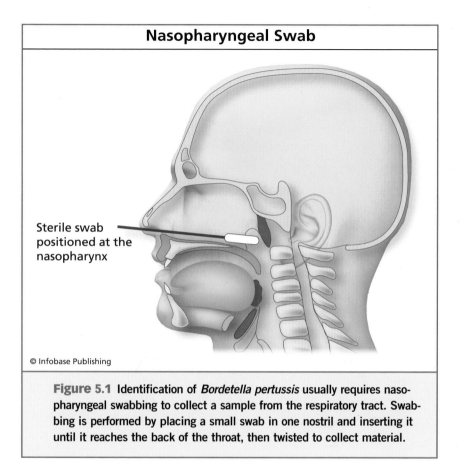

Sterile swab
positioned at the
nasopharynx

© Infobase Publishing

Figure 5.1 Identification of *Bordetella pertussis* usually requires naso-pharyngeal swabbing to collect a sample from the respiratory tract. Swab-bing is performed by placing a small swab in one nostril and inserting it until it reaches the back of the throat, then twisted to collect material.

to collect material and then withdrawn from the nostril. To increase the chances of collecting an appropriate specimen, the procedure is usually repeated in both nostrils. Either Dacron or calcium alginate swabs need to be used, as cotton contains fatty acids that can kill *B. pertussis*. Nasopharyngeal aspirates are collected in a similar manner; a narrow catheter is inserted into the nostril to the back of the throat, and a vacuum is applied to remove mucus and other material.

Once the specimen is collected, ideally it is immediately placed on a suitable medium for growth. Many smaller laboratories send specimens to a reference laboratory for culture of *B. pertussis*. In cases where there will be some time before a specimen can be plated, the swab or aspirate material is placed in Regan-Lowe transport medium or other suitable transport medium, and ideally kept at refrigerator temperature until the sample is ready to be plated on laboratory medium.[3]

Regan-Lowe charcoal agar, which is composed of 10 percent horse blood and the antibiotic cephalexin, is commonly used for the growth of *B. pertussis*. The charcoal binds to the fatty acids and other contaminants in the medium that may inhibit the growth of *B. pertussis*. The horse blood provides nutrients for the bacteria, and cephalexin inhibits the growth of most bacteria from the throat. *B. pertussis* is normally resistant to cephalexin, but because **susceptible** strains have occasionally been identified, frequently a plate of Regan-Lowe charcoal agar without cephalexin is also used for testing a clinical sample. Following inoculation, it takes from three to seven days for the bacteria to appear on the plate. The *B. pertussis* bacterial colonies have the appearance of little drops of mercury, or small pearls pressed into the surface of the medium.[4] Bacteria from these colonies are then Gram-stained. The presence of small, Gram-negative microbes is expected if the organism is *B. pertussis*. Often, additional tests are used to confirm the identification, such as biochemical tests or antibody or **polymerase chain reaction (PCR)** tests.

Another common method for identifying *B. pertussis* is to detect the microbe using antibody tests. The direct antibody technique is one example. This test can either be done directly on the material collected from a swab or from material aspirated from the nasopharynx. As the name suggests, this test involves using an antibody that binds directly to the bacteria. Typically the antibody is modified with a fluorescent dye, and a positive test occurs when fluorescently glowing bacteria are observed in the appropriate microscope. The direct antibody test must be performed in conjunction with another test, however, as the reliability of this test is quite variable.

Other antibody tests are performed on bacteria that have been grown on a culture plate. Often, an **agglutination test** is used. In this identification method, an antibody is added to a suspension of bacteria from an agar plate. The antibody causes visible clumping if *B. pertussis* is present.[5]

Another key method of identifying *B. pertussis* is detecting its DNA, using a technique called polymerase chain reaction (PCR). In some cases throat swabs work for identification of *B. pertussis* using PCR, so that is an advantage of this method, because collection using throat swabs is not as unpleasant for the patient as nasopharyngeal swabs. Once a sample potentially containing the bacteria has been collected, any bacterial cells that are present are isolated, and then treated to rupture the microbe and release its DNA. Specific small, single-stranded pieces of DNA are then added (primers) along with DNA polymerase, nucleotides, and buffer. Through a set of repeated heating and cooling cycles, large amounts of a particular section of DNA can be produced if *B. pertussis* is present, and this DNA can be readily detected. On the other hand, if *B. pertussis* DNA is not present, no new DNA will be produced, and the sample will be negative. In the most recently developed techniques this process can be automated, and a fluorescent signal will show if DNA is produced.[6] Although this technique can detect a very small number of organisms, it is possible to get false-positive reactions if the test is not conducted properly, so stringent methods to exclude DNA from previous reactions, and appropriate positive and negative controls are required.[7]

The tests described here focus on identifying the microbe responsible for the disease. Another diagnostic method relies on the reaction of the body to the presence of *B. pertussis*. In these cases, the testing is for the presence of antibodies in the blood of a person who is suspected of having whooping cough. The body produces specific antibodies in response to an infection, to *B. pertussis* in the case of whooping cough. These antibodies can be detected using an **enzyme-linked** immunosorbent assay (ELISA). Components of the bacterium are attached to small plastic wells in a test plate. Blood serum samples from the patient are then added to the test plate. If

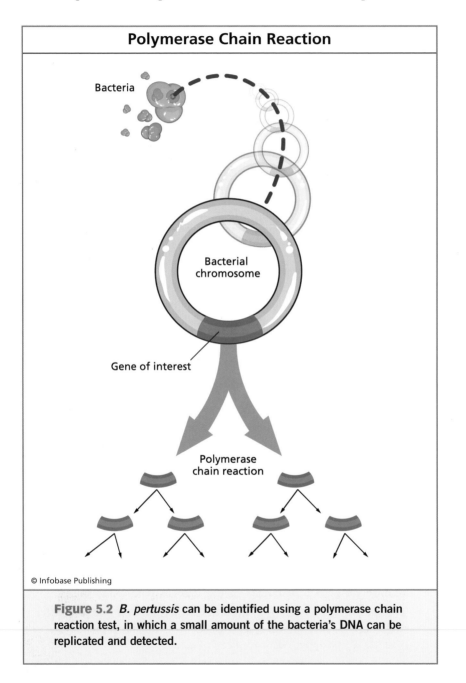

Polymerase Chain Reaction

Bacteria

Bacterial chromosome

Gene of interest

Polymerase chain reaction

© Infobase Publishing

Figure 5.2 *B. pertussis* can be identified using a polymerase chain reaction test, in which a small amount of the bacteria's DNA can be replicated and detected.

antibodies are present in the serum, they will attach to the bacterial components. Those antibodies can then be detected with a second antibody that contains an enzyme that will produce a color change when an appropriate substrate is added.

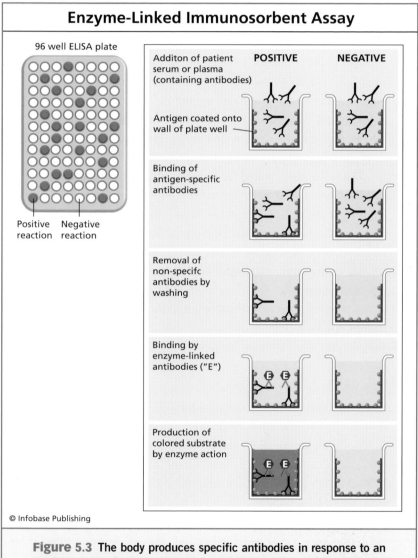

Figure 5.3 The body produces specific antibodies in response to an infection, or to *B. pertussis* in the case of whooping cough. These antibodies can be detected using an enzyme-linked immunosorbent assay (ELISA), enabling diagnosis of whooping cough.

FISH SCALES TO DETECT WHOOPING COUGH?

In 1988 and 1991, researchers from Sweden reported a novel method for detecting *Bordetella pertussis* infection using scales from the cuckoo wrasse *(Labrus ossifagus)*, a fish that is found off the Scandinavian coast. The findings were based on the observation that scales from this fish contain pigment deposits that are normally dispersed, but that clump together when exposed to the hormone noradrenalin. Pertussis toxin inhibits this clumping of these pigments, and at very low doses (about 1 part toxin in 100 trillion parts of a solution). Therefore one could use the fish scales to detect pertussis toxin, and thus the presence of *B. pertussis*.

The researchers tested 60 patients who had whooping cough using other diagnostic methods, including culture and antibody tests. In this "fish-scale assay," the saliva from 58 of these 60 positive patients tested positive for *B. pertussis* infection. This technique has not become widely adopted in clinical laboratories, although it is a simple test that might be useful in places with limited resources, as it only requires fish scales from an appropriate species, microscope slides, and a microscope.[8]

This testing is not very useful for diagnosis, since it takes one to two weeks for antibodies to develop following infection. However, testing for antibodies can help confirm an outbreak of whooping cough in an area.

CONDITIONS THAT CAN BE CONFUSED WITH WHOOPING COUGH

Because the initial symptoms of whooping cough are nonspecific, there are many other infections that might be confused with this ailment. For example, bronchitis and other respiratory infections can be caused by a variety of pathogens, including adenoviruses, parainfluenza virus, respiratory synctial virus, *Chlamydophila pneumonia,* and *Mycoplasma pneumonia.*[9] The treatments for whooping cough are different than the treatments used for these other microbes, so early diagnosis is important but challenging.

Many other respiratory conditions can be confused with whooping cough, particularly in adults who were vaccinated many years earlier, but are no longer immune. These conditions include asthma, chronic obstructive pulmonary disease, pneumonia, the common cold, tuberculosis, cystic fibrosis, and influenza.[10] In general, a diagnosis of whooping cough is made either through a change in symptoms (e.g., particularly the development of coughing fits) or through identification of the microbe in a nasopharyngeal specimen.

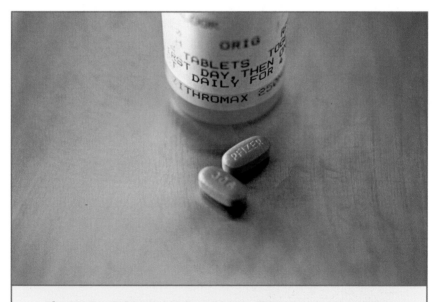

Figure 5.4 Azithromycin (brand name Zithromax) is one antibiotic commonly prescribed for treatment of whooping cough. (Michelle Del Guerci/Photo Researchers Inc.)

TREATMENTS

As described in the chapter on the history of whooping cough, early treatments for the disease were limited, ineffective, and often dangerous. Yet even today, the most current treatments do not offer relief during all stages of the infection, and there is still a need for improvements in the treatments that are used.

One group of treatments is designed to simply minimize symptoms. These would include the use of oxygen for patients who become blue during coughing fits, suctioning of the respiratory tract to remove airway obstruction, and providing sufficient liquid and nutrients (through an intravenous line, if necessary) to replace food and water lost through vomiting.

TOXIN RELEASE FOLLOWING ANTIBIOTIC TREATMENT

Antibiotics are powerful weapons in the war against bacterial pathogens. On rare occasions, antibiotics, even when working properly, could temporarily worsen symptoms of disease. For example, in the case of whooping cough a substantial fraction of pertussis toxin remains inside the bacterial cell as it grows in the body. There was a concern that if antibiotics broke open the bacterial cells, they therefore cause the amount of pertussis toxin in the body to increase.

Researchers from the University of Cincinnati tested the release of pertussis toxin from *Bordetella pertussis* in the presence or absence of different antibiotics. They found that the amount of pertussis toxin released was somewhat greater two hours after exposure to several antibiotics, compared to those cells not exposed to any antibiotic. However, after 24 hours the bacteria exposed to the antibiotic released much less pertussis toxin. Therefore, although in the short term there was some additional toxin released, the antibiotics ultimately appear to limit the production of toxin.[11]

THE COST OF TREATING WHOOPING COUGH

Researchers from Massachusetts analyzed of the cost of hospital treatment for whooping cough in the United States from 1996 to 1999. Based on an analysis of cases in California, Florida, Massachusetts, and Washington they estimated a mean cost of $9,130 per hospital stay. Extrapolating to the United States as a whole, the cost of hospital treatment for whooping cough per year is about $17 million (in 2002 dollars). Considering that the true costs of whooping cough include outpatient treatment for many patients, and indirect costs such as lost wages, the actual yearly cost is likely to be significantly larger than $17 million.[12]

Antibiotics are the primary drug treatment for whooping cough. Erythromycin and chemically related drugs, such as azithromycin, are widely used for treating whooping cough.[13] Erythromycin and related drugs have a good safety record and can reach high concentrations in the respiratory tract. Ideally, the antibiotics should be taken early in the course of an infection. Once a patient develops severe coughing spells, there is not a clear indication that taking an antibiotic reduces the severity of symptoms or the duration of their illness. Taking an appropriate course of antibiotics (from five to 14 days, depending on the antibiotic) can reduce the risk of transmitting the disease to others, however.[14]

Until the mid-1990s there had not been a documented case of erythromycin-resistant *B. pertussis*.[15] Subsequently, there have been several reports of erythromycin-resistant strains, although they still appear to be rare.[16] Molecular analysis of resistant strains showed that they had a single nucleotide change in the ribosome, which is part of the cellular protein manufacturing machinery. This region of the ribosome normally binds to erythromycin.[17] This suggests that the drug resistance was based on selection of resistant mutants rather than, for example, transfer of an antibiotic resistance gene from one strain to another.

OTHER TREATMENTS

Once symptoms develop, there are very few options for treatment other than supportive care. Several drugs have been employed for treatment, including antihistamines and steroids, but controlled studies have not confirmed that these drugs are effective in reducing symptoms. **Pertussis immunoglobulin** has been studied to treat cases of whooping cough, but without much effectiveness.[18] This medication contains antibodies directed against *B. pertussis* proteins, which likely blunts the action of toxins, and increases the ability of the immune system to destroy the microbe.

6

Prevention of Whooping Cough

In 2004 two infants in a London neonatal intensive care unit developed whooping cough. One infant had only received two vaccinations for whooping cough, and the other had not received any whooping cough vaccinations. Following treatment, both babies recovered. Since whooping cough is a relatively uncommon illness, the clustering of these two cases led to an investigation of whether there was a common source that had caused both of these infections. One nurse, who worked in the unit where the babies stayed, had developed a severe cough a few weeks earlier, but continued working in the neonatal unit. Testing showed that she had a high concentration of antibodies in her blood that reacted strongly to Bordetella pertussis, *suggesting a recent infection. This nurse, and all the other health care workers in the unit, were given a seven-day course of antibiotics. No further cases were subsequently reported. This case study highlights the importance of vaccination against whooping cough at an early age, and also the increased frequency with which adults and teenagers transmit whooping cough to infants.*[1]

The primary method of preventing whooping cough is through vaccination. The first whooping cough vaccine was developed shortly after the isolation of *Bordetella pertussis* in 1906, although it took several decades before vaccines with consistently high potency and limited side effects were developed.

By the 1940s vaccination had begun in the United States, and by the 1950s whooping cough vaccines were widely administered. The effects of vaccination were dramatic. The peak number of whooping cough deaths

Figure 6.1 The primary means of preventing whooping cough is through vaccination. Three doses of vaccine are recommended by six months of age. (James Gathany/Centers for Disease Control and Prevention)

in the United States occurred in 1923, when 9,269 people, mostly infants, died. By 2006 the number of whooping cough deaths had dropped to 27, a greater than 99 percent decrease in deaths. Similarly, the number of cases dropped from more than 200,000 in the 1930s to about 15,000 presently.[2]

WHOLE CELL VACCINE

In the development of the original whooping cough vaccine, a number of strategies were employed to ensure that the vaccine caused a sufficient immune response while minimizing harmful side effects. One of the parameters that varied were the conditions under which the microbes were grown. Eventually, it became clear that the production of key factors critical for immunity (such as pertussis toxin and filamentous hemaglutinin) occurred at the highest levels with relatively freshly grown strains that were cultured in the proper medium (e.g., media containing high levels of proteins). In addition, the number and concentration of bacteria included in the preparation also affected the usefulness of the vaccine. In general, the larger the number of bacteria, the better the immune response, but the greater potential for side effects. Early attempts to develop effective whole-cell vaccines included a range of 50 million to 140 billion bacteria per vaccine dose.[3] Recently developed vaccines consist of approximately 10 billion *B. pertussis* cells per

Number of Reported Pertussis Cases, by Year— in the United States from 1922 to 2005

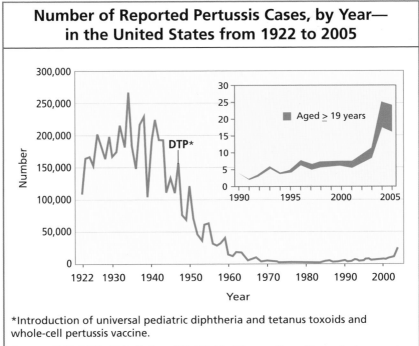

*Introduction of universal pediatric diphtheria and tetanus toxoids and whole-cell pertussis vaccine.

Source: 1950-2005, CDC, National Notifiable Diseases Surveillance System, and 1922-1949, passive reports to the Public Health Service

© Infobase Publishing

Figure 6.2 The introduction of the whooping cough vaccine starting in the early 1940s led to a rapid decline in cases.

vaccine dose.[4] Other researchers experimented with a variety of methods for the inactivation of the bacteria in a way that still appropriately stimulated the immune system. This work continued into the recent past. A 1987 report from researchers in India tested vaccines that had been inactivated with the mercury compound thimerosal, formaldehyde, gluteraldehyde, acetone, or heat. According to this report, thimerosal best preserved the ability of the bacteria to induce an immune response.[5]

In 1942 the whooping cough vaccine was combined with the diphtheria and tetanus vaccines by Dr. Pearl Kendrick; combining the vaccines minimizes the total number of vaccinations required, and enhances compliance with the vaccination schedule, since fewer individual vaccinations would be required. It was also found that the whooping cough vaccine enhanced the effectiveness of the vaccinations against diphtheria and tetanus. Newer combined vaccines, such as Pentacel and Pediarix, protect against an even larger range of pathogens, including diphtheria, tetanus, whooping cough, hepatitis B, and polio.[6]

ACELLULAR PERTUSSIS VACCINE

Depending on the manufacturer, the acellular pertussis vaccine consists of one or more antigens from *B. pertussis*. These are proteins that are isolated after growing the bacteria in a particular type of microbiological medium. For example, one type of vaccine, Infantrix from GlaxoSmithKline, contains inactivated pertussis toxin (inactivated with formaldehyde and gluteraldehyde) and inactivated filamentous hemaglutinin and peractin (both inactivated with formaldehyde).[7] Another manufacturer, Sanofi Pasteur, produces an accellular vaccine with the same components listed above, plus fimbrae isolated from bacterial cells.[8] Clinical studies indicated that three doses of this acellular vaccine provided about 85 percent protection against clearly defined whooping cough infections.[9]

Currently, most of the vaccines for whooping cough simultaneously protect against diphtheria, tetanus, and whooping

Table 6.1. Recommended DTaP Vaccine Schedule in the United States, 2009[11]

2 months	4 months	6 months	15–18 months	4–6 years	11–12 years
DTaP	DTaP	DTaP	DTaP	DTaP	Tdap
Source: Centers for Disease Control and Prevention					

cough (DTaP vaccine for children, then Tdap for adolescents and adults). (Tetanus is caused by the bacterium *Clostridium tetani*; diphtheria is caused by the bacterium *Corynebacterium diphtheriae*.) This vaccine consists of the diphtheria toxin, which has been attenuated by treatment with heat and formaldehyde. The vaccine also contains tetanus toxin, which has been rendered harmless by a similar treatment process.[10] As noted above, newer vaccines include the DTaP vaccine, plus some additional antigens for hepatitis B and polio. Vaccination for pertussis in the United States currently involves a set of six injections prior to the age of 12 with a catch-up vaccination during the teen years or during adulthood if a person did not get a whooping cough booster after age 11. The DTaP vaccine, used during childhood, contains larger amounts of antigen directed against all three microbes to ensure a strong immune response. The Tdap vaccine, given to adolescents, contains lower amounts of antigen for diphtheria and whooping cough to boost protection against infection, while minimizing side effects. This adolescent vaccine was recommended due to an increased number of cases of whooping cough in adolescents, as well as in the population as a whole.

PROTECTION FROM DIFFERENT VACCINES

There is some evidence that the acellular vaccines induce a different type of immune response (more antibody production, less cellular immunity), as compared with the whole-cell

Consequence of Pertussis Vaccination and Drop-Off in Vaccination Rate in England and Wales

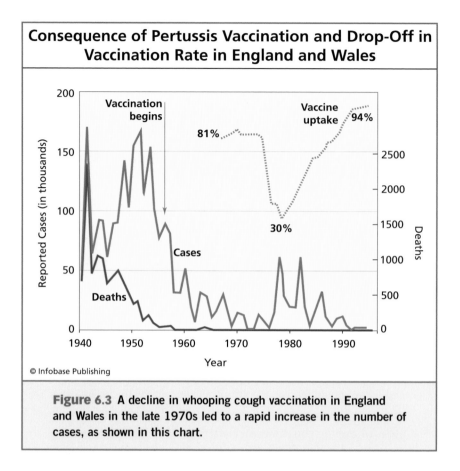

© Infobase Publishing

Figure 6.3 A decline in whooping cough vaccination in England and Wales in the late 1970s led to a rapid increase in the number of cases, as shown in this chart.

vaccine. This could result in a less effective or shorter duration of immunity. One follow-up study designed to answer this question produced encouraging results, however. It compared the immune response of teenagers to a booster dose of an acellular vaccine, based on whether they received acellular or whole-cell vaccines as children. The researchers, from two German institutions, found that the immune responses were similar in both groups, regardless of which vaccine they had previously received. One cautionary note is that it is unclear to what extent the patients had inapparent whooping cough infections following their last vaccination. If this was common, it would have provided a natural enhancement of the immunization they previously received, and would make the results more difficult to interpret.[12] There is also ongoing research to ensure that the components of the vaccine produce optimal strong and long-lasting immunity. For example, there is some evidence that some of the components of *B. pertussis*, such as filamentous hemaglutinin, may dampen the immune response. Consequently, work is underway to determine whether some of these components should be omitted from the acellular vaccines.

VACCINE SIDE EFFECTS

All medical treatments have some risk associated with them. Although vaccines are generally considered to be very safe, side effects do sometimes occur.[13] For example, with the DTaP vaccine mild side effects occur in up to one-third of children within a few days of receiving the shot. These side effects include:

- fever, along with pain, swelling, and/or redness at the site of injection

- tiredness and fussiness

- swelling of the entire arm (in about 1 child in 30; more often after the fourth or fifth dose of vaccine)

- vomiting (in about 1 child in 50)

Generally these symptoms pass without any treatment or further complications. In some ways, these side effects are actually a positive sign, in that they suggest that the immune system is reacting to the vaccine in a way that will engender defense against these diseases. Moderate side effects are rare and include the following:

- nonstop crying for three hours or more (1 child in 1,000)

- seizures—jerking or staring (1 child in 14,000)

- fever over 105°F (1 child in 16,000)

Although serious and of great concern to caregivers, these symptoms normally pass without the need for treatment (beyond the use of a non-aspirin pain reliever to treat fever). Severe reactions to the vaccine are very rare. Severe effects that have been linked to the vaccine include serious allergic reactions, which are reported in less than one case per million. Other severe ailments that have occurred after vaccination include permanent brain damage and long-term seizures. However, these have occurred so rarely that no clear link has been made between the vaccine and these conditions.

Another vaccine (DTwP), composed of whole *B. pertussis* cells, along with diphtheria and tetanus toxoids, had a higher rate of vaccine side effects (about 26 reports per 100,000 vaccinations versus about 12 per 100,000 with DTaP). Following studies that showed the DTaP vaccine was effective at preventing these three diseases, only DTaP and Tdap (which is also acellular) have been recommended for immunization in the United States from 2000 onward.[14]

VACCINE CONTRAINDICATIONS

Based on an analysis of vaccine side effects, it is recommended that the vaccine *not* be administered in the following cases:

- a child with a moderate or severe illness (the vaccination should wait until they recover)
- a child with a severe allergic reaction to a previous dose of the vaccine
- a child who developed disease of the central nervous system within a week after a previous DTaP vaccination

Parents should consult with their physician about the advisability of vaccination in the following situations:

- a child cried for three hours or more following vaccination
- a child developed a fever of 105°F following vaccination
- a child had seizures following vaccination[15]

VACCINE SAFETY

While no medical intervention is without some risks, perhaps the best way of evaluating the risk from a pertussis vaccine is to compare the likelihood of serious harm from taking the vaccine to the likelihood of harm from not taking the vaccine. Experts predict that without vaccination the United States would annually have approximately 185,000 cases and 4,000 deaths due to pertussis each year. Examining the United States' Vaccine Adverse Events Reporting System (VAERS) data for 2006, there were eight deaths reported that occurred shortly after a DTaP vaccine was given.[16] Possibly, none of these deaths were actually caused by the vaccine. However, assuming the unlikely worst-case scenario that all these deaths were caused by the vaccine, the benefits are still about 500:1 in favor of a lower risk of death from vaccination, as compared with the risk of death if the vaccine was not used.

It is important to be aware that the VAERS system collects voluntary reports of vaccine side effects from health care providers, patients, and others. Because the reports are not required, there is the possibility that complications of vaccination, including death, may be underreported. However, another study indicated that very serious reactions, such as seizures, were very likely to be entered into the VAERS; this suggests that most, if not all, of the vaccine-associated deaths would have been reported.[17]

COMPENSATION FOR INJURY

To provide a mechanism for compensating patients who have a serious adverse reaction to vaccination, the United States has established a National Vaccine Injury Compensation Program.[18] Currently, for the DTaP vaccine, the serious complications for which compensation is available include:

- Anaphylaxis or anaphylactic shock within four hours of receiving the shot. This is a severe allergic reaction to the vaccine that can cause death as a result of airway blockage. Based on a study by scientists at research institutions and hospitals on the West Coast of the United States,[19] the risk of anaphylaxis for childhood vaccines is less than 1 per million doses of vaccine. Although serious, if recognized quickly this reaction can easily be treated in most medical settings. In this study, none of the anaphylactic reactions were fatal.

- Brachial neuritis, a nervous system disorder that normally starts with a deep, severe pain in the arm and shoulder and eventually leads to muscle weakness in the upper body. Based on a study of side effects in infants, it appears that brachial neuritis occurs in this age group at a rate well below 1 case per 15 million doses.[20] In most patients, recovery from brachial neuritis begins within a month after symptoms appear, and 90 percent of patients had completely recovered after three years.[21]

As the number of serious vaccine-preventable diseases has declined in developed countries, a perception has arisen among some individuals that vaccines are more dangerous than the diseases they are intended to prevent. There have been claims that certain diseases are associated with specific vaccines. In many cases, these claims have not held up to scrutiny. For example, there have been some concerns about a possible link between vaccines and autism, and a particular concern based on the use of a mercury-based preservative, thimerosal, in vaccines. Although current medical and scientific evidence does not support a link between the use of this preservative and autism or other illness, thimerosal was removed from childhood vaccines in the United States in 2001.[22] In very rare cases, serious illness can follow vaccination. There may be a small number of individuals who are genetically predisposed to react to a component of a vaccine. Additional research will help answer whether other ailments may also be associated with the DTaP vaccine, aside from those listed above. Public health authorities emphasize that the benefits of vaccination greatly outweigh the risks, however.[23]

In particular, the DTaP vaccine is considered by public health experts to be among the safest vaccines, since the vaccine consists of only specific components that are involved in causing disease in humans, and not whole microbes. As a result, there are fewer components in the vaccine, thus reducing the risk of side effects.

There is both an element of personal benefit and social good involved in receiving vaccinations for communicable diseases. By having a large proportion of the population vaccinated, an epidemic is less likely to spread, which offers additional protection both to those who are not and those who cannot be vaccinated. This is particularly a concern for infants and young children, who are most susceptible to developing a severe case of whooping cough. Most often, they get infected through contact with teenagers or adults who have whooping cough, but do not show the classical symptoms.

One challenge for health care providers is to communicate the information about the value of vaccination effectively to nervous parents. There has been a long history of anti-vaccination groups, dating back at least to the late 1800s. In part, these groups responded to a concern about individual rights in the face of mandatory vaccination. At present, these groups are able to rapidly disseminate information via the Internet, and much of what is found on anti-vaccination Web sites is based on individual stories of bad outcomes attributed to vaccines. Countering this information is a challenge for health care providers who may have the statistics and data on their side, but not compelling personal stories.[24]

One claim that is often made by vaccine opponents is that improved sanitation and other public health measures rather than vaccines were responsible for the decrease in deaths due to whooping cough (and other diseases) in the twentieth century. Some of the clearest evidence arguing against this viewpoint comes from data showing a dramatic increase in cases of whooping cough following reduced levels of vaccination in several countries. The increases in cases occurred over a short period of time, and there was no indication of other changes in public health during the time that fewer children received whooping cough vaccinations. For example, the whole-cell whooping cough vaccine was withdrawn from medical practice in Sweden in 1979, due to concerns about side effects. By 1994 there were 13,142 cases of whooping cough in Sweden. Once an acellular whooping cough vaccine was reintroduced in 1996, the incidence of whooping cough dropped by more than 80 percent within two years, to only 1,463 cases in 1998.[25]

VACCINE EFFECTIVENESS

The proportion of people who are protected from whooping cough through vaccination varies with the number of vaccinations received, and the time since the last vaccination. According to a 2005 report from a group of researchers from the Centers for Disease Control and Prevention, a single vaccination with the whole-cell whooping cough vaccine was 80–85 percent effective at preventing whooping cough. Three vaccinations reduced the risk of whooping cough by almost 96 percent, and four vaccinations reduced the risk of whooping cough by almost 98 percent during the first five years of life.[26] As noted above, a clinical study suggested that one brand of the acellular vaccine was about 85 percent effective in preventing whooping cough after three doses.[27]

CURRENT VACCINE RESEARCH

One area of active research involves developing an improved vaccine for whooping cough. As noted above, the current vaccine is not exceptionally effective, and the duration of protection is not very long (six to 10 years). Consequently, there have been a number of efforts to develop a more long-lasting vaccine that produces fewer side effects.

One example of these efforts is the production of a genetically modified, inactive pertussis toxin, which requires minimal chemical inactivation. This toxoid is apparently more similar in shape to the natural toxin, and it therefore leads to the production of a more natural and effective immune response.[28]

Other advances being tested to enhance vaccination include improved **adjuvants**. (Adjuvants are chemicals that

ADMINISTERING VACCINES

Traditionally, vaccination involves going to the doctor and getting an injection with a needle and syringe. This method of administering vaccines has been an effective and efficient way of preventing many diseases. However, in addition to the concerns of people who are shy around needles, vaccination with traditional shots might not always the best way to induce an appropriate immune response.

For some diseases, ingestion of a vaccine may induce stronger and longer-lasting immunity. This approach has been employed in the oral polio vaccine; ingestible vaccines are also being developed for a wide range of infections of the gastrointestinal tract, such as cholera. One strategy being considered as a way of producing inexpensive oral vaccines is to genetically engineer plants to produce a vaccine. In some cases, simply eating the plant could confer immunity to a particular disease.

Another possible strategy for administering vaccines is through nasal sprays or inhalers. A vaccine that induces a strong immune response in the nose, throat, and lungs might provide better protection from respiratory infections. FluMist is a commercially available nasal spray vaccine for preventing influenza, which is a respiratory disease. A nasal spray vaccine is an attractive option for whooping cough, because the bacterium infects the respiratory tissues. A nasal vaccination for whooping cough has been tested in mice, and research is currently underway to develop a similar vaccine for preventing whooping cough in humans.

enhance the response to vaccination.) For example, a study in mice, reported in 2007 by researchers in Nova Scotia, Canada, showed that a single injection of the DTaP vaccine, containing an improved adjuvant, protected mice as well as three injections of the DTaP vaccine lacking a new adjuvant.[29] In another approach designed to make a whooping cough vaccine that would stimulate a stronger immune response, the same group of Nova Scotia researchers tested a vaccine made of a genetically combined fragment of pertussis toxin and cholera toxin. The portions of the toxins used were not harmful, but they could induce a strong immune response. In particular, the cholera toxin is capable of binding to the surface of cells lining the respiratory tract. This made this strategy of coupling the pertussis toxin and cholera toxin together a possible means for developing a vaccine that could be administered by spraying an aerosol vaccine into the nose or throat. In tests in mice, the combined toxins, administered by this route, offered protection from aerosolized *B. pertussis*.[30]

VACCINE STRATEGIES

Among vaccine-preventable diseases, whooping cough has been the most difficult to control, and the number of cases has gone up in many countries since the 1970s. This has several possible explanations. For example, improved diagnosis and reporting of whooping cough, waning immunity following vaccination, mutations in strains of *B. pertussis* that make them less affected by vaccine-induced immune responses, and less transmission of whooping cough, which makes it less likely that people will continue to be exposed to this microbe and remain immune, have all been proposed as explanations.[31] None of these explanations entirely fit all the available evidence, but three strategies have been proposed to reduce the incidence of whooping cough, based on these hypotheses. One strategy involves the production of an improved vaccine, which is described earlier in the chapter. Particularly if this vaccine produces a longer-lasting immunity, that could lead to a substantial reduction in the number of cases of whooping cough, since a larger fraction of the population would be protected from infection for a longer period of time.

A second strategy would include using an increased number of booster shots to continue to maintain immunity in the population. This strategy has been adopted in the United States and other countries, where Tdap booster shots are now recommended for preteens, health-care workers, and new moms. It is not clear yet how effective this approach will be in reducing the number of cases of whooping cough. A review of a number of recent studies found support for the idea that a booster vaccination for adolescents and adults decreased the overall number of whooping cough cases. The results were not definitive, however, and the cost per case of whooping cough prevented appeared to be fairly high.[32] In addition, the cost of additional vaccinations, the lack of awareness of the prevalence of whooping cough in many places, and an inability to easily diagnose whooping cough have made it difficult to implement a strategy that includes more booster shots at later ages, at least in some countries.[33] In contrast, one study of people in the Northwest Territories, Canada, showed a dramatic decrease in cases following the implementation of an adult vaccination for whooping cough.[34]

A third strategy involves vaccination of specific groups that are most likely to transmit whooping cough to infants, since infants are most likely to suffer severely and even die from infection. For example, vaccination of mothers who have low levels of antibodies to whooping cough may be one useful strategy for reducing whooping cough in infants. The evidence supporting this strategy is limited, but some studies have shown infants to be protected from whooping cough for six months, if their mothers were vaccinated during pregnancy. This is because the mother transfers her antibodies to the fetus; in addition, antibodies can also be transmitted to infants via breast milk. Some

LACK OF VACCINATION IN CONFLICT ZONES

Afghanistan has been in a state of conflict since 2001, when the country was invaded by the United States and a coalition of other countries. Subsequently, several investigations were conducted to determine vaccination coverage and the incidence of whooping cough in the country. In one report researchers from Japan studied the vaccine coverage for diphtheria, tetanus, and whooping cough (DPT), in different parts of Afghanistan. Not surprisingly, they found that the areas that had the highest levels of conflict had the lowest levels of vaccine coverage. For example, in 2003, 144 districts (about 45 percent of the country) had a DPT immunization rate below 50 percent. Although this was a substantial improvement from 2000, when about three-quarters of the country had a vaccination rate for DPT below 50 percent, vaccination rates below 80 percent make a population vulnerable to whooping cough epidemics.[35]

Researchers from a university in Pakistan subsequently reported data they had collected on whooping cough incidence in Afghanistan between March 2007 and March 2008. They collected data from hospitals and clinics where people came in with suspected cases of whooping cough. A team then went in to verify those cases. During this one-year period, the researchers confirmed more than 700 cases of whooping cough and 32 deaths. This is a greater number of deaths due to whooping cough than recently reported in the United States, which has approximately 10 times the population of Afghanistan; this means that the death rate for whooping cough is at least 10 times higher in Afghanistan than in the United States.[36] A lack of security is therefore likely to contribute to low vaccination rates, and consequently higher rates of disease and death.

additional data needs to be collected (for example, whether vaccination of the mother reduces the effectiveness of vaccination in infants) before vaccination of mothers becomes widely used in medical practice.[37]

7

Future Prospects and Concerns Regarding Whooping Cough

In a 2007 report physicians and researchers at Vanderbilt University, along with the Tennessee Department of Health and the Centers for Disease Control and Prevention, analyzed data from 37 students at Vanderbilt who had a cough of more than two weeks' duration. Primarily through antibody tests, they determined that 10 of these students (27 percent) had, in fact, recently suffered from whooping cough. A larger mail survey of students at Vanderbilt University confirmed the widespread nature of a whooping cough outbreak at the school. Sixty-six of 225 students (29 percent) who returned the survey described a recent illness that had them coughing for at least two weeks. The high prevalence of whooping cough in this specific incident mirrors an emerging trend of whooping cough becoming more and more common in adolescents and adults in developed countries around the world.[1]

INCIDENCE OF PERTUSSIS IN VACCINATED PEOPLE

Of all the vaccine-preventable illnesses, whooping cough is the least well controlled. In the United States in 2004, more than 25,000 cases were reported; other estimates that include a range of cases indicate that the number may actually be as high as 600,000 cases per year in the United States.[2] Currently, more than 90 percent of children in the United States have been vaccinated with at least three shots to prevent whooping cough.

Consequently, most cases are now in young infants who have not yet received at least three shots, and in adolescents and adults whose immunity has waned since they were last vaccinated.

EFFECT OF VACCINATION ON *B. PERTUSSIS* STRAINS

Vaccination represents a stiff challenge to bacterial pathogens. Highly effective vaccination can stop the transmission of a pathogen, threatening it with extinction. Therefore, any pathogen strains that can evade a vaccine-induced immune response will tend to become more common in the population. This is particularly a concern for the newer acellular vaccines, which only contain a few bacterial antigens. A mutation in *Bordetella pertussis* that leads to a change in a single antigen could, hypothetically, allow the microbe to at least partially evade the immune response generated by these acellular vaccines.

There is some evidence this has happened with whooping cough vaccination in some countries. The strains of *B. pertussis* that have been isolated following vaccination in an area share some mutations that were not found prior to vaccination. These mutations affected two key virulence proteins (peractin and pertussis toxin). Experiments in mice demonstrated that these mutant strains have an enhanced ability to grow in animals that had been vaccinated, compared to strains that were widely distributed prior to vaccination.[3]

Researchers from France studied strains of *B. pertussis* in France and Senegal that were isolated between 1991 and 1995. The strains from France represented selection to evade vaccine-induced immunity after several decades of vaccination, meaning that current strains in France were different from those found before widespread vaccination. In contrast, the strains from Senegal represented strains from an area with little vaccination, and therefore showed little selection against *B. pertussis* strains similar to vaccine strains. They found that the dominant strain in Senegal was similar to the *B. pertussis* strains found in France prior to widespread vaccination. The current strains in France and Senegal produced different antigens, likely reflecting a selection against proteins found in the vaccines used in France.[4]

In a similar way, a report from Germany showed that following the use of an acellular vaccine the number of *B. pertussis* infections dropped substantially. The number of infections by a related, but less virulent organism—*B. parapertussis*—increased dramatically, however. This suggested the vaccine selected against *B. pertussis*, and therefore provided a niche for the growth of this other *Bordetella* species. [5]

Another report from researchers in France, showed that recently isolated strains of *B. pertussis* from areas with a long history of vaccination tend to contain fewer genes than the strains that were present prior to the widespread use of vaccination. This study did not find evidence of *B. pertussis* acquiring new genes in response to selection caused by vaccination.[6] Similar results were reported from researchers in Finland.[7] Other workers had also shown a change in the key antigens in strains of *B. pertussis* in response to vaccination in Sweden[8] and Russia.[9] It is not yet clear to what extent these changes in the genomes of *B. pertussis* may have on the protection conferred by vaccination.

SEQUENCE OF *BORDETELLA PERTUSSIS* GENOME
In 2003 the complete sequence of *B. pertussis*, along with the sequences of the closely related microbes *B. bronchiseptica* and *B. pertussis*, was reported by a group of scientists from England, the United States, and Germany.[10] As described previously, *B. pertussis* is closely related to *B. bronchiseptica*, and its **genome** (the sum of all the microbe's genetic material) is about 20 percent smaller than the ancestral genome of *B. bronchiseptica*. This has occurred primarily through the spread of insertion sequences throughout the genome of *B. pertussis*, which in turn has led to deletions and a reduction in the total number of genes. That reduction varies somewhat between

different strains, but a rough estimate is that *B. pertussis* has about 25 percent fewer genes (about 1,200 fewer) compared to the common ancestor it shared with *B. bronchiseptica*. In addition to deletions, these insertion sequences also caused genome rearrangements, and these are widespread in the *B. pertussis* genome, when it is compared with *B. bronchiseptica*.

Many of the genes that are no longer found in *B. pertussis* encode surface proteins. These are likely to be recognized by the immune system, so the loss of these proteins might protect the microbe from antibodies and other protective mechanisms that might otherwise eliminate the organism from the body. This reduction in the number of genes has most likely had two effects: narrowing the host range of *B. pertussis* to just humans,

CAN PERTUSSIS BE ERADICATED?

The fact that humans are the only known host for *B. pertussis* infection leads to hope that the microbe can be eradicated. At the same time, the relatively short duration of protection against whooping cough afforded by the current vaccine, and the widespread nature of the disease across the globe makes complete eradication a difficult and complex prospect.

One idea that has been advanced is to give adults DTaP vaccines every 10 years rather than just the "T" vaccine for tetanus. Potentially, this would provide sufficient immunity within the population to protect infants from the disease, and could eventually lead to elimination of whooping cough. Of course, the development of a vaccine that provided lifelong immunity after a single shot would be even more likely to be effective; it is not clear if this is possible, however, and the incentives for pharmaceutical companies developing vaccines would work against this type of immunization. Therefore, for biological and economic reasons, it is not yet clear whether whooping cough can ever be completely eliminated.[11]

and reducing the ability of B. pertussis to survive for extended periods in the environment.[12]

There is some concern that the strain used for the original sequencing reaction is not representative of B. pertussis strains, particularly those that have been circulating since the implementation of widespread vaccination. The strain of B. pertussis that was sequenced, Tohama I, was originally isolated in the 1950s, just as vaccination was becoming widespread. A report from French researchers showed that in many cases more recent strains have had deletions of their genomes, which have significantly reduced the number of genes present in some of these strains, compared to the Tohama I strain. There was also at least one region missing in the Tohama I strain that was present in most other B. pertussis strains. Consequently, sequencing a single strain of bacteria, particularly for widespread human pathogens, probably does not capture all the important genetic diversity of these microbes.[13]

FUTURE PROSPECTS

There is still a great deal that we need to know about whooping cough. For example, in spite of the vast amount of research that has been conducted, the basis of the distinctive cough in pertussis is not yet clear. Further study of the proteins produced by B. pertussis might reveal additional toxins that are responsible for the fits of coughing that are associated with the disease.

Better models of disease also need to be developed. Although several useful animal models exist for whooping cough, none of them fully replicates the disease in humans. In the absence of this type of animal model, it is much more difficult to understand the molecular basis of whooping cough, and to develop effective treatments for the disease.

Although great strides have been made in developing safer whooping cough vaccines, additional work is required to maximize the ability of these vaccines to provide long-term protection against infection. For example, it might be necessary to add additional antigens to the acellular vaccines to ensure maximum protection and to be sure that none of the components dampen the immune response.

There is also a need to better understand how prevalent whooping cough really is. One advance that would be very helpful is a simple, inexpensive diagnostic test that would readily detect *B. pertussis* infection. A test like this would allow for studies that could clearly delineate the pattern of transmission of whooping cough in the population and help contribute to the development of public health measures to control the disease.[14]

Whooping cough remains an important disease, both in the United States and around the world. Although much progress has been made in controlling whooping cough, a great deal of additional research will be required to ensure that we can universally prevent and treat this serious ailment.

Notes

Chapter 1

1. S. Bonacorsi et al., "Treatment Failure of Nosocomial Pertussis Infection in a Very-Low-Birth-Weight Neonate," *Journal of Clinical Microbiology* 44, 10 (2006): 3830–3832.
2. R. Sinha and P. Heath, "Pertussis," *Medicine* 33, 5 (2005): 101–102.
3. J. Cunha, "Whooping Cough," eMedicine, http://www.emedicinehealth.com/whooping_cough/article_em.htm (accessed November 30, 2008).
4. J. Bocka, "Pediatrics, Pertussis," eMedicine, http://www.emedicine.com/EMERG/topic394.htm (accessed November 30, 2008).
5. S. Mattoo and J. Cherry, "Molecular Pathogenesis, Epidemiology, and Clinical Manifestations of Respiratory Infections Due to *Bordetella pertussis* and Other *Bordetella* Subspecies," *Clinical Microbiology Reviews* 18, 2 (2005): 326–382.
6. A. van der Zee et al., "A Clinical Validation of *Bordetella pertussis* and *Bordetella parapertussis* Polymerase Chain Reaction: Comparison with Culture and Serology Using Samples from Patients with Suspected Whooping Cough from a Highly Immunized Population," *Journal of Infectious Disease* 174 (1996) : 89–96.
7. O. Bjornstad and E. Harvill, "Evolution and Emergence of Bordetella in Humans," *Trends in Microbiology* 13, 8 (2005): 355–359.
8. T. Eidlitz-Markus and A. Zeharia, "Adolescent Pertussis-Induced Partial Arousal Parasomnia," *Pediatric Neurology* 35, 4 (2006): 264-267.
9. E. Bamberger and I. Srugo, "What Is New in Pertussis?," *European Journal of Pediatrics* 167 (2008): 133–139.
10. E. Bamberger and I. Srugo, "What Is New in Pertussis?," *European Journal of Pediatrics* 167 (2008): 133–139.
11. S. Roush, T. Murphy, and the Vaccine-Preventable Disease Table Working Group, "Historical Comparisons of Morbidity and Mortality for Vaccine-Preventable Diseases in the United States," *Journal of the American Medical Association* 298, 18 (2007): 2155–2163. E.Weir, "Resurgence of *Bordetella pertussis* infections," *Canadian Medical Association Journal* 167, 10 (2002): 167.
12. Centers for Disease Control and Prevention, "Vaccine Preventable Deaths and the Global Immunization Vision and Strategy, 2006–2015," *Morbidity and Mortality Weekly Report* 55, 18 (2006): 511–515. World Health Organization, "Pertussis Surveillance," https://www.who.int/vaccines-documents/DocsPDF01/www605.pdf (accessed November 30, 2008).
13. T. Eidlitz-Markus and A. Zeharia, "*Bordetella pertussis* as a Trigger of Migraine without Aura," *Pediatric Neurology* 33 (2005): 283–284.

Chapter 2

1. J. L. Smith, *A treatise on the diseases of infancy and childhood* (Philadelphia: Lea Brothers and Company, 1892), 432.
2. D. Diavatopoulos et al., "*Bordetella pertussis*, the Causative Agent of Whooping Cough, Evolved from a Distinct, Human-Associated Lineage of *B. bronchiseptica*," *Public Library of Science Pathogens* 1 (2005): e45.
3. F. Versteegh, et al., "Pertussis: a Concise Historical Review including Diagnosis, Incidence, Clinical Manifestations and the Role of Treatment and Vaccination in Management," *Reviews in Medical Microbiology* 16 (2005): 79–89.
4. W. Holmes, *Bacillary and Rickettsial Infections* (New York: The Macmillan Co., 1940), 675.
5. J. L. Smith, *A Treatise on the Diseases of Infancy and Childhood* (Philadelphia: Lea Brothers and Company, 1892), 432.
6. J. Lapin, *Whooping Cough* (Springfield, Ill.: Charles Thomas, 1943), 3.
7. F. Versteegh, et al., "Pertussis: a Concise Historical Review including Diagnosis, Incidence, Clinical Manifestations and the Role of Treatment and Vaccination in Management," *Reviews in Medical Microbiology* 16 (2005): 79–89.

8. J. L. Smith, *A Treatise on the Diseases of Infancy and Childhood* (Philadelphia: Lea Brothers and Company, 1892), 432.

9. J. Lapin, *Whooping Cough* (Springfield, Ill.: Charles Thomas, 1943), 3.

10. C. Meigs, *Observations on Certain of the Diseases of Young Children* (Philadelphia: Lea and Blanchard, 1850), 159.

11. J. L. Smith, *A Treatise on the Diseases of Infancy and Childhood* (Philadelphia: Lea Brothers and Company, 1892), 431.

12. J. L. Smith, *A Treatise on the Diseases of Infancy and Childhood* (Philadelphia: Lea Brothers and Company, 1892), 432.

13. M. Hatfield, *The Acute Contagious Diseases of Childhood* (Chicago: G.P. Engelhard and Company, 1901) 82.

14. H. Lechevalier and M. Solotorovsky, *Three Centuries of Microbiology,* (New York: McGraw-Hill Book Company, 1974), 246.

15. A. Petterson, "Presentation Speech," (presentation speech for the Nobel Prize in Physiology or Medicine, Stockholm, Sweden, December 10, 1920), http://nobelprize.org/nobel_prizes/medicine/laureates/1919/press.html (accessed

16. M. Pittman, "Symposium on Pertussis: Evaluation and Research on Acellular Pertussis Vaccines," *Developments in Biological Standards* 73 (1990): 13–29.

17. D. Geier and M. Geier, "The True Story of Pertussis Vaccination. A Sordid Legacy?," *Journal of the History of Medicine and Allied Sciences* 57 (2002): 249–284.

18. H. MacDonald and E. MacDonald, "Experimental Pertussis," *The Journal of Infectious Diseases* 53 (1933): 328–330.

19. M. Pittman, "Symposium on Pertussis: Evaluation and Research on Acellular Pertussis Vaccines," *Developments in Biological Standards* 73 (1990): 13–29; D. Geier and M. Geier, "The True Story of Pertussis Vaccination. A Sordid Legacy?," *Journal of the History of Medicine and Allied Sciences* 57 (2002): 249–284.

20. S. Matto and S. and J. Cherry, "Molecular Pathogenesis, Epidemiology, and Clinical Manifestations of Respiratory Infections Due to *Bordetella pertussis* and Other *Bordetella* Subspecies," *Clinical Microbiology Reviews,* 18, 2 (2005): 326–382.

21. D. Geier and M. Geier, "The True Story of Pertussis Vaccination. A Sordid Legacy?," *Journal of the History of Medicine and Allied Sciences* 57 (2002): 249–284.

22. E. Mellish, "Bromoform in the Treatment of Pertussis," in *The Chicago Medical Reporter*, Vol. II (Chicago: W.T. Keener, 1891–1892), 427.

23. Environmental Protection Agency, "Bromoform," http://www.epa.gov/ttn/atw/hlthef/bromofor.html (accessed June 27, 2009).

24. PTCL Safety Web Site "Safety Data for Phenol," http://msds.chem.ox.ac.uk/PH/phenol.html (accessed February 28, 2009).

25. R. Kemp, *Diseases of the Stomach, Intestines, and Pancreas* (Philadelphia: W.B. Saunders and Company, 1917) 234.

26. T. Kilmer, "Whooping Cough. A Study of 18 Cases Treated with the Elastic Abdominal Belt," *Medical Record* 65 (1904): 983.

27. J. L. Smith, *A Treatise on the Diseases of Infancy and Childhood* (Philadelphia: Lea Brothers and Company, 1892), 441–443.

28. E. Ingalls, *Diseases of the Chest, Throat, and Nasal Cavities,* (New York: William Wood and Company, 1898), 155.

29. J. Wilson, *Modern Clinical Medicine, Infectious Diseases* (New York: D. Appleton and Company, 1911) 786–787.

Chapter 3

1. "Fourteen Cases of Whooping Cough in Beltrami County," *Bemidji Pioneer Newspaper,* January 13, 2009.

2. S. Elahi, J. Holmstrom, and V. Gerdts, "The Benefits of Using Diverse Animal Models for Studying Pertussis," *Trends in Microbiology* 15, 10 (2007): 462-468.

3. H. MacDonald and E. MacDonald, "Experimental pertussis," *The Journal of Infectious Diseases* 53 (1933): 328–330.

4. J. Cunha, "Whooping Cough," eMedicine, http://www.emedicinehealth.

com/whooping_cough/article_em.htm (accessed November 30, 2008).

5. C. Kerley, *Treatment of the Diseases of Children*. 2d ed. (Philadelphia: W.B. Saunders, 1909), 226.

6. M. Seema and J. Cherry, "Molecular Pathogenesis, Epidemiology, and Clinical Manifestations of Respiratory Infections Due to *Bordetella pertussis* and Other *Bordetella* Subspecies," *Clinical Microbiology Reviews* 18, 2 (2005): 326–382.

7. C. Vanderpool and S. Armstrong, "The *Bordetella bhu* Locus Is Required for Heme Iron Utilization," *Journal of Bacteriology* 183, 14 (2001): 4278-4287.

8. M. Seema and J. Cherry, "Molecular Pathogenesis, Epidemiology, and Clinical Manifestations of Respiratory Infections Due to *Bordetella pertussis* and Other *Bordetella* Subspecies," *Clinical Microbiology Reviews* 18, 2 (2005): 326–382.

9. S. Hellwig et al., "Immunoglobulin A-Mediated Protection against *Bordetella pertussis* Infection," *Infection and Immunity* 69, 8 (2001): 4846–4850.

10. K. Mills, "Immunity to *Bordetella pertussis*," *Microbes and Infection* 3 (2001): 655–677.

11. K. Mills, "Immunity to *Bordetella pertussis*," *Microbes and Infection* 3 (2001): 655–677.

12. S. Paccani et al., "Suppression of T-Lymphocyte Activation and Chemotaxis by the Adenylate Cyclase Toxin of *Bordetella pertussis*," *Infection and Immunity* 76, 7 (2008): 2822–2832.

13. K. Mills, "Immunity to *Bordetella pertussis*," *Microbes and Infection* 3 (2001): 655–677.

14. C. Williams, R. Haines, and P. Cotter, "Serendipitous Discovery of an Immunoglobulin-Binding Autotransporter in Bordetella Species," *Infection and Immunity* 76, 7 (2008): 2966–2977.

15. S. Paccani et al., "Suppression of T-Lymphocyte Activation and Chemotaxis by the Adenylate Cyclase Toxin of *Bordetella pertussis*," *Infection and Immunity* 76, 7 (2008): 2822–2832; J.

Shumilla et al., "*Bordetella pertussis* Infection of Primary Human Monocytes Alters HLA-DR Expression," *Infection and Immunity* 72, 3 (2004): 1450–1462.

16. M. Barnes and A. Weiss, "BrkA Protein of *Bordetella pertussis* Inhibits the Classical Pathway of Complement after C1 Deposition," *Infection and Immunity* 69, 5 (2001): 3067–3072.

17. S. Elahi, J. Holmstrom, and V. Gerdts, "The benefits of using diverse animal models for studying pertussis," *Trends in Microbiology* 15, 10 (2007): 462-468.

18. C. Cummings et al., "Species- and Strain-Specific Control of a Complex, Flexible Regulon by *Bordetella* BvgAS," *Journal of Bacteriology* 188, 5 (2006): 1775–1785.

19. C. Cummings et al., "Species- and Strain-Specific Control of a Complex, Flexible Regulon by *Bordetella* BvgAS," *Journal of Bacteriology* 188, 5 (2006): 1775–1785.

20. M. Mishra et al., "The BvgAS Signal Transduction System Regulates Biofilm Development in *Bordetella*" *Journal of Bacteriology* 187, 4 (2005): 1474-1484.

21. C. Vanderpool and S. Armstrong, "Integration of Environmental Signals Controls Expression of *Bordetella* Heme Utilization Genes," *Journal of Bacteriology* 186, 4 (2004): 938–948.

Chapter 4

1. P. Guilfoile, *Tetanus* (New York: Chelsea House Publishers, 2008).

2. I. Henderson et al., "Type V Protein Secretion Pathway: the Autotransporter Story," *Microbiology and Molecular Biology Reviews*, 68 (2004): 692–744.

3. M. Seema and J. Cherry, "Molecular Pathogenesis, Epidemiology, and Clinical Manifestations of Respiratory Infections Due to *Bordetella pertussis* and Other *Bordetella* Subspecies," *Clinical Microbiology Reviews* 18, 2 (2005): 326–382.

4. S. Backert and T. Meyer, "Type IV Secretion Systems and Their Effectors

in Bacterial Pathogenesis," *Current Opinion in Microbiology* 9 (2006): 207–217.

5. N. Dautin, G. Karimova, and D. Ladant, "*Bordetella pertussis* Adenylate Cyclase Toxin: A Versatile Screening Tool," *Toxicon* 40 (2002): 1383–1387.

6. J. Loucká et al., "Delivery of a MalE CD4-T-Cell Epitope into the Major Histocompatibility Complex Class II Antigen Presentation Pathway by *Bordetella pertussis* Adenylate Cyclase, *Infection and Immunity* 70, 2 (2002): 1002–1005.

7. T. Stenson, A. Patton, and A. Weiss, "Reduced Glutathione Is Required for Pertussis Toxin Secretion by *Bordetella pertussis*," *Infection and Immunity* 71 (2003): 1316–1320.

8. M. Seema and J. Cherry, "Molecular Pathogenesis, Epidemiology, and Clinical Manifestations of Respiratory Infections Due to *Bordetella pertussis* and Other *Bordetella* Subspecies," *Clinical Microbiology Reviews* 18, 2 (2005): 326–382.

9. M. Seema and J. Cherry, "Molecular Pathogenesis, Epidemiology, and Clinical Manifestations of Respiratory Infections Due to *Bordetella pertussis* and Other *Bordetella* Subspecies," *Clinical Microbiology Reviews* 18, 2 (2005): 326–382.

Chapter 5

1. M. Hatfield, *The Acute Contagious Diseases of Childhood* (Chicago: G.P. Engelhard and Company, 1901), 89.

2. Centers for Disease Control and Prevention, "1997 Pertussis (Whooping cough) Case Definition," http://www.cdc.gov/ncphi/disss/nndss/casedef/pertussis_current.htm (accessed April 12, 2009).

3. M. Loeffelholz, "Bordetella," in *Manual of Clinical Microbiology*, 8th ed., eds. P. Murray et al. (Washington, D.C.: American Society for Microbiology Press, 2003), 614–625.

4. P. Engelkirk and J. Duben-Engelkirk, *Laboratory Diagnosis of Infectious Diseases* (Baltimore: Lippincott, Williams, and Wilkins, 2008) 335.

5. M. Loeffelholz, "Bordetella." in *Manual of Clinical Microbiology*, 8th ed., eds. P. Murray et al. (Washington, D.C.: American Society for Microbiology Press, 2003), 614–625.

6. L. Knorr et al., "Evaluation of Real-time PCR for Diagnosis of *Bordetella pertussis* Infection," *BMC Infectious Diseases* 6 (2006): 62.

7. M. Loeffelholz, "Bordetella," in *Manual of Clinical Microbiology*, 8th ed., eds. P. Murray et al. (Washington, D.C.: American Society for Microbiology Press, 2003), 614–625.

8. J. Karlsson et al.,"The Melanophore Aggregating Response of Isolated Fish Scales: A Very Rapid and Sensitive Diagnosis of Whooping Cough," *FEMS Microbiology Letters* 66, 2 (1991): 169–75; R. Andersson et al., "A Rapid and Sensitive Assay for Pertussis Toxin Based on Pigment Aggregation with the Melanophores of an Isolated Fish Scale," *FEMS Microbiology Letters* 55 (1988): 191–194.

9. M. Loeffelholz, "Bordetella." in *Manual of Clinical Microbiology*, 8th ed., eds. P. Murray et al. (Washington, D.C.: American Society for Microbiology Press, 2003), 614–625.

10. J. Bocka, "Pediatrics, Pertussis," eMedicine, http://www.emedicine.com/EMERG/topic394.htm (accessed November 30, 2008).

11. K. Craig-Mylius and A. Weiss, "Antibacterial Agents and Release of Periplasmic Pertussis Toxin from *Bordetella pertussis," Antimicrobial Agents and Chemotherapy* 44 (2000): 1383–1386.

12. J. O'Brien and J. Caro, "Hospitalization for Pertussis: Profiles and Case Costs by Age," *BioMed Central Infectious Diseases* 5 (2005): 57–66.

13. E. Hewlett, "Bordetella Species" in *Principles and Practices of Infectious Diseases,* 4th ed., eds. G. Mandell, J. Bennett, and R. Dolin (New York: Churchhill Livingston, 1994), 2078–2084; R. Srinivasan and T. Yeo, "Are Newer Macrolides Effective in Eradicating Carriage of Pertussis?," *Archives of Disease in Childhood* 90 (2005): 322–324.

14. R. Srinivasan and T. Yeo, "Are Newer Macrolides Effective in Eradicating Carriage of Pertussis?," *Archives of Disease in Childhood* 90 (2005): 322–324.

15. E. K. Korgenski and J. A. Daly, "Surveillance and Detection of Erythromycin Resistance in *Bordetella pertussis* Isolates Recovered from a Pediatric Population in the Intermountain West Region of the United States," *Journal of Clinical Microbiology* 35 (1997): 2989–2991.

16. K. Gordon et al., "Antimicrobial Susceptibility Testing of Clinical Isolates of *Bordetella pertussis* from Northern California: Report from the SENTRY Antimicrobial Surveillance Program, *Antimicrobial Agents and Chemotherapy* 45, 12 (2001): 3599–3600; K. Wilson et al., "*Bordetella pertussis* Isolates with a Heterogeneous Phenotype for Erythromycin Resistance," *Journal of Clinical Microbiology* 40, 8 (2002): 2942–2944.

17. J. Bartkus et al., "Identification of a Mutation Associated with Erythromycin Resistance in *Bordetella pertussis*: Implications for Surveillance of Antimicrobial Resistance," *Journal of Clinical Microbiology* 41, 3 (2003): 1167–1172.

18. S. A. Halperin et al., "Is Pertussis Immune Globulin Efficacious for the Treatment of Hospitalized Infants with Pertussis?" *Pediatric Infectious Disease Journal* 26, 1 (2007): 79–81.

Chapter 6

1. E. Alexander et al., "Pertussis Outbreak on a Neonatal Unit: Identification of a Healthcare Worker as the Likely Source," *Journal of Hospital Infection* 69 (2008): 131–134.

2. S. Roush and T. Murphy, "Historical Comparisons of Morbidity and Mortality for Vaccine-Preventable Diseases in the United States and the Vaccine-Preventable Disease," *Journal of the American Medical Association* 298, 18 (2007): 2155–2163.

3. J. Lapin, *Whooping Cough* (Springfield, Ill: Charles Thomas, 1943), 158–160.

4. Lederle Laboratories, Tetramune vaccine package insert, http://whale.to/m/tetramune.html (accessed March 22, 2009).

5. R. Gupta et al., "The Effects of Different Inactivating Agents on the Potency, Toxicity, and Stability of Pertussis Vaccine," *Journal of Biological Standardization* 15, 1 (1987): 87–98.

6. GlaxoSmithKline Biologicals, "Pediarix prescribing information," http://us.gsk.com/products/assets/us_pediarix.pdf (accessed on March 22, 2009).

7. Food and Drug Administration,"Infantrix package insert," http://www.fda.gov/Cber/label/infanrixLB.pdf (accessed March 21, 2009).

8. Food and Drug Administration, "DAPTACEL package insert," http://www.fda.gov/Cber/label/daptacelLB.pdf (accessed March 21, 2009).

9. Food and Drug Administration,"Infantrix package insert," http://www.fda.gov/Cber/label/infanrixLB.pdf (accessed March 21, 2009); Food and Drug Administration, "DAPTACEL package insert," http://www.fda.gov/Cber/label/daptacelLB.pdf (accessed March 21, 2009).

10. Centers for Disease Control and Prevention, "2009 Childhood and Adolescent Immunization Schedule," http://www.cdc.gov/vaccines/recs/schedules/downloads/child/2009/09_0-6yrs_schedule_pr.pdf, http://www.cdc.

gov/vaccines/recs/schedules/downloads/child/2009/09_7-18yrs_schedule_pr.pdf (accessed March 21, 2009).

11. Centers for Disease Control and Prevention, "Pertussis Vaccination: Use of Acellular Pertussis Vaccines Among Infants and Young Children Recommendations of the Advisory Committee on Immunization Practices (ACIP)," *Morbidity and Mortality Weekly Report* 46, RR-7 (1997): 1–25.

12. N. Rieber et al., "Differences of Humoral and Cellular Immune Response to an Acellular Pertussis Booster in Adolescents with a Whole Cell or Acellular Primary Vaccination," *Vaccine* 26 (2008): 6929–6935.

13. Centers for Disease Control and Prevention,"Diphtheria, Pertussis, and Tetanus Vaccines: What You Need to Know," http://www.cdc.gov/vaccines/pubs/vis/downloads/vis-dtap.pdf (accessed March 31, 2008).

14. B. Song and R. Katial, "Update on Side Effects from Common Vaccines," *Current Allergy and Asthma Reports* 4 (2004): 447–453.

15. Centers for Disease Control and Prevention,"Diphtheria, Pertussis, and Tetanus Vaccines: What You Need to Know," http://www.cdc.gov/vaccines/pubs/vis/downloads/vis-dtap.pdf (accessed March 31, 2008).

16. Vaccine Adverse Event Reporting System (VAERS), CDC WONDER Online Database, http://wonder.cdc.gov/vaers.html (accessed March 22, 2009).

17. S. Rosenthal and R.T. Chen, "The Reporting Sensitivities of Two Passive Surveillance Systems for Vaccine Adverse Events," *American Journal of Public Health* 85, 12 (1995): 1706–1709.

18. U.S. Health and Human Services, "Vaccine Injury Compensation Table," http://www.hrsa.gov/vaccinecompensation/table.htm (accessed April 3, 2008).

19. K. Bohlke et al., "Risk of Anaphylaxis After Vaccination of Children and Adolescents," *Pediatrics* 112 (2003): 815–820.

20. M. Braun et al., and the VAERS Working Group, "Infant Immunization with Acellular Pertussis Vaccines in the US: Assessment of the First Two Years' Data from the Vaccine Adverse Event Reporting System (VAERS)," *Pediatrics* 106 (2000): e51.

21. L. Dillin, F. Hoaglund, and M. Scheck, "Brachial Neuritis," *The Journal of Bone and Joint Surgery* 7 (1985): 878-880.

22. Centers for Disease Control and Prevention, "Mercury and Vaccines (Thimerosal)," http://www.cdc.gov/od/science/iso/concerns/thimerosal.htm (accessed March 31, 2008).

23. Centers for Disease Control and Prevention, "History of Vaccine Safety," http://www.cdc.gov/od/science/iso/basic/history.htm (accessed March 31, 2008).

24. S. Blume, "Anti-vaccination Movements and Their Interpretations," *Social Science and Medicine* 62 (2006): 628–642.

25. P. Olin and H. O. Hallander, "Marked Decline in Pertussis Followed Reintroduction of Pertussis Vaccination in Sweden," *Eurosurveillance* 4, 12 (1999), http://www.eurosurveillance.org/ViewArticle.aspx?ArticleId=84 (accessed April 25, 2009).

26. K. Bisgard et al., and the Pertussis Investigation Team, "Pertussis Vaccine Effectiveness Among Children 6 to 59 Months of Age in the United States, 1998–2001," *Pediatrics* (2005) 116: e285–e294.

27. Food and Drug Administration, "DAPTACEL package insert," http://www.fda.gov/Cber/label/daptacelLB.pdf (accessed March 21, 2009).

28. J. Robbins et al., "The rise in pertussis cases urges replacement of chemically-inactivated with genetically-inactivated toxoid for DTP," *Vaccine* 25 (2007): 2811–2816.

29. M. Mansour et al. "Improved Efficacy of a Licensed Acellular Pertussis Vaccine, Reformulated in an Adjuvant Emulsion of Liposomes in Oil, in a Murine Model," *Clinical and Vaccine Immunology* 14, 10 (2007): 1381–1383.

30. S. Lee et al., "Mucosal Immunization with a Genetically Engineered Pertussis Toxin S1 Fragment-Cholera Toxin Subunit B Chimeric Protein," *Infection and Immunity* 71, 4 (2003): 2272–2275.

31. R. Aguas, G. Goncalves, and M. G. Gomes, "Pertussis: Increasing Disease as a Consequence of Reducing Transmission," *Lancet Infectious Disease* 6 (2006): 112–117.

32. I. Rodriguez-Cobo et al., "Clinical and Economic Assessment of Different General Population Strategies for Pertussis Vaccine Booster Regarding Number of Doses and Age of Population for Reducing Whooping Cough Disease Burden: A Systematic Review," *Vaccine* 26 (2008): 6768–6776.

33. K. Forsyth et al., "Pertussis Immunization in the Global Pertussis Initiative International Region. Recommended Strategies and Implementation Considerations," *Pediatric Infectious Diseases Journal* 24 (2005): S93–S97.

34. K. Kandola et al., "A Comparison of Pertussis Rates in the Northwest Territories: Pre- and Post-acellular Pertussis Vaccine Introduction in Children and Adolescents," *Canadian Journal Infectious Diseases & Medical Microbiology* 16, 5 (2005): 271–274.

35. T. Mashal et al., "Impact of Conflict on Infant Immunisation Coverage in Afghanistan: a Countrywide Study 2000–2003," *International Journal of Health Geographics* 6 (2007): 23–32.

36. R. Kakar, M. Mojadidi, and J. Mofleh, "Pertussis in Afghanistan, 2007–2008," *Emerging Infectious Diseases* 15, 3 (2009): 501.

37. F. Mooi and S. de Greeff, "The Case for Maternal Vaccination against Pertussis," *Lancet Infectious Disease* 7 (2007): 614–624.

Chapter 7

1. A. Craig et al. "Outbreak of Pertussis on a College Campus," *The American Journal of Medicine* 120 (2007): 364–368.

2. J. Cunha, "Whooping Cough," eMedicine, http://www.emedicinehealth.com/whooping_cough/article_em.htm (accessed November 30, 2008).

3. G. Gandona and T. Day, "Evidences of Parasite Evolution after Vaccination," *Vaccine* 26S (2008): C4–C7.

4. E. Njamkepo et al., "Genomic Analysis and Comparison of *Bordetella pertussis* Isolates Circulating in Low and High Vaccine Coverage Areas," *Microbes and Infection* 10 (2008): 1582–1586.

5. J. Liese et al., and The Munich Vaccine Study Group, "Clinical and Epidemiological Picture of *B. pertussis* and *B. parapertussis* infections after introduction of acellular pertussis vaccines," *Archives of Disease in Childhood* 88 (2003): 684–687.

6. V. Bouchez et al. "Genomic Content of *Bordetella pertussis* Clinical Isolates Circulating in Areas of Intensive Children Vaccination," *PLoS ONE* 3, 6 (2008): e2437.

7. E. Heikkinen et al., "Comparative Genomics of Bordetella pertussis Reveals Progressive Gene Loss in Finnish Strains," *PLoS ONE* 2, 9 (2007): e904.

8. H. Hallander et al., "Shifts of *Bordetella pertussis* Variants in Sweden from 1970 to 2003,

during Three Periods Marked by Different Vaccination Programs," *Journal of Clinical Microbiology* 43, 6 (2005): 2856–2865.

9. O. Borisova et al., "Antigenic Divergence between *Bordetella pertussis* Clinical Isolates from Moscow, Russia, and Vaccine Strains," *Clinical and Vaccine Immunology* 14, 3 (2007): 234–238.

10. J. Parkhill et al., "Comparative Analysis of the Genome Sequences of *Bordetella pertussis, Bordetella parapertussis,* and *Bordetella bronchiseptica*," *Nature Genetics* 35, 1 (2003): 32–40.

11. A. Preston, "*Bordetella pertussis*: the Intersection of Genomics and Pathobiology,"

Canadian Medical Association Journal 173, 1 (2005): 55–62.

12. A. Preston, "*Bordetella pertussis*: the Intersection of Genomics and Pathobiology," *Canadian Medical Association Journal* 173, 1 (2005): 55–62.

13. V. Caro, V. Bouchezc, and N. Guiso, "Is the Sequenced *Bordetella pertussis* Strain Tohama I Representative of the Species?," *Journal of Clinical Microbiology* 46, 6 (2008): 2125–2128.

14. S. Mattoo, S. and J. Cherry, "Molecular Pathogenesis, Epidemiology, and Clinical Manifestations of Respiratory Infections Due to *Bordetella pertussis* and Other *Bordetella* Subspecies," *Clinical Microbiology Reviews*, 18, 2 (2005): 326–382.

Glossary

acellular vaccine—A vaccine that does not contain whole cells, but rather individual components. In the case of the acellular whooping cough vaccine, individual molecules such as inactivated pertussis toxin are used.

adaptive immune response—An immune response that develops in response to a specific pathogen. It consists of molecules including antibodies and cells including B cells and cytotoxic T lymphocytes.

adhesins—Molecules, usually on the surface of a microbe, that allow it to bind to other cells. In *B. pertussis* filamentous hemagglutinin is an example of an adhesin.

adjuvants—Chemicals that are used to enhance the immune response to vaccination. Currently, the only approved adjuvant in the United States is alum (aluminum hydroxide) but others are being tested for safety and increased effectiveness.

agglutination test—A commonly used test to detect the presence of bacterial or viral pathogens. An antibody to a specific pathogen is added to a suspension of a microbe. If the microbe is the specific pathogen that reacts to the antibody, there will be a visible clumping of the solution, allowing for pathogen identification.

antibodies—Proteins produced by a type of immune system cell called a B cell. Antibodies bind to antigens, either to the surface of the microbe, or to toxins or other molecules released by the microbes. The binding of antibodies to these antigens usually inhibits their function and enhances the ability of the body to destroy the pathogen or the molecules the pathogen secretes.

antigen—A molecule, frequently a protein, which induces the production of, and is bound by, antibodies. Typically, pathogens like *B. pertussis* contain multiple antigens.

bronchioles—The smallest of the thin-walled air passages in the lungs, which end in the small sac-like structures called alveoli.

calmodulin—A human protein that activates pertussis toxin and adenylate cyclase toxin. In the cell the normal function of calmodulin is to bind to calcium and regulate the activity of calcium-dependent enzymes.

capsule—A coating on the outer surface of bacteria, typically consisting of carbohydrates. This coating makes it difficult for immune system cells to engulf and destroy the bacterial cells.

CD4+ T cell—A cell of the immune system that controls immune responses to pathogens including *B. pertussis*.

cellular immune response—A specific immune response involving cytotoxic T lymphocytes, which home in on and destroy cells that are infected with a pathogen.

ciliated cells—Cells lining the respiratory tract that have finger-like projections on their surface, called cilia. The cilia move in a coordinated manner, allowing for the removal of mucus and foreign matter from the respiratory tract.

complement—A group of proteins that constantly circulate in the bloodstream. These proteins become activated in response to the signals that indicate a bacterial infection. As a result, the complement proteins are deposited on the surface on the bacteria, enhancing the ability of immune system cells to ingest the bacteria. In addition, complement proteins can form pores in bacterial membranes, which are lethal to the microbes.

contagious—Capable of spreading disease.

cytotoxic T cells—A type of immune system cell that attacks and destroys human cells infected with viruses or bacteria.

dendritic cell—An immune system cell that can ingest, process, and display antigens from pathogens. These antigens, present on the surface of dendritic cells, then activate other cells of the immune system. Dendritic cells are closely related to macrophages.

DNA sequence—A determination of the exact sequence of individual components of a DNA molecule (abbreviated A, C, G, T). This sequence can be used to identify genes, and to infer the genetic relationship between organisms.

enzyme linked immunosorbent assay (ELISA)—A diagnostic test, usually used to determine if specific antibodies to a particular pathogen are present. In an ELISA test, blood serum is taken from a patient and added to wells containing antigens. If the blood serum contains antibodies directed against the pathogen, they will bind and can be detected. A positive test means that the person either has or has had the disease, or at least has been exposed to the pathogen.

endotoxins—Poisons produced by bacterial cells that normally remain part of the bacterial cell. A component of the bacterial cell envelope in Gram-negative bacteria, lipopolysaccharide, is the most common endotoxin.

exotoxins—Poisons produced by bacterial cells that are excreted. These toxins are normally proteins, and typically exert their effect by gaining entry into host cells.

fimbriae—Hairlike protein projections on the surface of bacterial cells that allow the microbes to bind to human cells.

flagella—Long, whip-like structures on the surface of bacterial cells that allow bacteria to move in liquids.

genome—The complete genetic makeup of an organism. Genome sequencing has allowed for a comparison of all the genes from organisms such as those that cause whooping cough and related disease organisms.

G proteins—Regulatory proteins in human cells that are involved in controlling many intracellular processes. Toxins, such as pertussis toxin, target G-proteins and prevent them from functioning. This causes disruption of the cells and often, death of the cells.

Gram negative—One of the major categories of bacteria, distinguished by its pink color when treated with a series of stains and chemicals. The presence of an inner and outer membrane, separated by a thin cell wall, is responsible for the staining characteristics of these microbes.

hemoglobin—The oxygen-carrying protein in the blood that contains iron. Hemoglobin is often a source of iron for bacteria that are growing in the body.

hemolysins—Toxins produced by bacteria that are characterized based on their ability to break open red blood cells.

immune system—The system in the body that fights infections.

infectious—Capable of being transmitted from one infected individual to another. An infectious disease is caused by a microbe that can be passed from an infected person to a susceptible person.

innate immune response—Molecules and cells in the body that are always present, and capable of responding to any infection. The innate immune response includes complement and cells such as macrophages and neutrophils.

macrophages—A type of cell involved in the innate immune system, which engulfs and destroys many types of bacterial pathogens. Macrophages sit in the tissues and respond to bacterial pathogens in their environment.

neutrophils—A type of cell involved in the innate immune system, which engulfs and destroys many types of bacterial pathogens. Neutrophils typically circulate in the bloodstream and move into a site of infection in response to chemical signals.

paroxysm—A spasm-like fit of, for example, uncontrolled coughing. A paroxysmal cough is one of the characteristic symptoms of whooping cough.

periplasm—A space between the inner and outer membrane of Gram-negative bacterial cells. The presence of a periplasm means that the transport of proteins out of Gram-negative bacteria requires additional steps.

pertussis immunoglobulin—A treatment for severe whooping cough that involves infusing serum that contains high levels of antibodies to *B. pertussis*.

phagocytic cells—Cells of the immune system, including macrophages, dendritic cells, and neutrophils, which ingest and destroy foreign material in the body, such as *B. pertussis* pathogens.

pili—Small hairlike projections on the surface of bacterial cells that are frequently involved in attachment to mammalian cells.

polymerase chain reaction (PCR)—A technique for amplifying a small section of DNA. This method is used for, among other things, detecting bacterial DNA, such as from *B. pertussis*, to determine if the microbe is present at the site of an infection. The reaction consists of DNA from the pathogen, DNA primers, DNA polymerase, nucleotides, and a buffer.

protease—A type of enzyme that cuts proteins into smaller pieces.

reduced glutathione—A chemical produced by cells in the body that acts as an antioxidant, protecting cells and tissues from the byproducts of metabolic reactions. It consists of three amino acids: cysteine, glutamate, and glycine. Reduced glutathione is abundant in certain parts of the body, like the respiratory tract, that are likely to have high levels of exposure to potentially damaging oxygen compounds.

susceptible—Capable of being infected, usually because a person has not been vaccinated, or because they have not had the disease previously.

toxins—Molecules, typically proteins, that act as biological poisons.

Type III secretion system—A mechanism for transferring bacterial proteins inside a human or other eukaryotic cell. The system itself consists of proteins that form a needle-like complex in the membrane of the bacterial cell. This needle-like complex then acts as the conduit for transferring the proteins.

virulence factors—Molecules, usually proteins, which enable a pathogen to grow and survive inside the body.

Further Resources

Books and Articles

Brown, K. P. Cassiday, M. Lucia Tondella, A. Cohn, and Kris Bisgard. "Pertusiss." In *Manual for the Surveillance of Vaccine-Preventable Diseases*. 4th ed. Atlanta: Centers for Disease Control and Prevention, 2008. Available online. URL: http://www.cdc.gov/vaccines/Pubs/surv-manual/chpt10-pertussis.htm.

Crowcroft, N., and J. Britto. "Whooping cough—a continuing problem." *British Medical Journal* 324 (2002): 1537–1538.

Crowcroft, N., and R. Pebody. "Recent Developments in Pertussis." *Lancet* 367 (2006): 1926–1936.

Forsyth, K. "Pertussis, Still a Formidable Foe." *Clinical Infectious Diseases* 45 (2007): 1487–1489.

Web Sites

Centers for Disease Control and Prevention: Pertussis
http://www.cdc.gov/ncidod/dbmd/diseaseinfo/pertussis_t.htm

eMedicine: Pediatrics, Pertussis
http://emedicine.medscape.com/article/803186-overview

Mayo Clinic: Pertussis
http://www.mayoclinic.com/health/whooping-cough/DS00445

Todar's Online Textbook of Bacteriology: *Bordetella pertussis* and whooping cough
http://www.textbookofbacteriology.net/pertussis.html

Whooping Cough.Net
http://www.whoopingcough.net/welcome.htm

Index

chloroform, 26
cholera toxin, 80
chronic obstructive
    pulmonary disease, 63
ciliated cells, 9, 36, 55
Clostridium tetani, 71
cocaine, 27. *See also*
    whooping cough,
    treatments
cold, common, 63
communicable diseases, 6
complement (blood
    component), 33, 41,
    43–44
contagious disease, 30
convalescent stage, 30
*Corynebacterium
    diphtheriae*, 71
coughing fits, 8–9, 30, 64
cresoline, 27. *See also*
    whooping cough,
    treatments
Creutzfeldt-Jakob disease
    (vCJD), 6
cuckoo wrasse, 62
cyclic AMP, 52, 54
cystic fibrosis, 63
cytotoxic T cells, 42

Dacron swabs, 57
de Ballon, Guillanne, 19
dendritic cells, 42
dermonecrotic toxin, 35,
    55
diarrheal infection, 6
diphtheria, 70, 71, 82
diphtheria, tetanus, and
    whooping cough (DPT)
    vaccine coverage, 82
DNA, 12, 46, 59
Doull, James, 24
DPT vaccine coverage. *See*
    diphtheria, tetanus, and
    whooping cough
    vaccine coverage
drug resistance, 65–66
drugs. *See* anti-infective
    drugs; *specific drugs*

DtaP vaccine, 71, 74, 76–77,
    80, 87. *See also*
    vaccination
DTwP vaccine, 74. *See also*
    vaccination

Ebola fever, 6
eelshusten, 19. *See also*
    whooping cough
Eldering, Grace, 23, 25
endotoxins, 48, 55
energy metabolism, 46
enzyme-linked immuno-
    sorbent assay (ELISA),
    59–62
erythromycin, 65–66
Europe, 15, 18
exotins, 48
eyes, inflamed, 9

Faroe Islands, Scotland, 22
FHA. *See* filamentous
    hemaglutinin
filamentous hemaglutinin
    (FHA), 30, 34, 39, 43,
    46, 68–69, 70, 73
fimbriae, 33, 34, 39, 46, 70
fish scale assay, 62
flagella, 37
FluMist, 79
Fur, 47

genetic regulation of
    virulence, 45–57
Gengou, Octave, 21, 22
genome, 86–88
GlaxoSmithKline, 70
glutathione, 53
G proteins, 49
Gram-negative bacteria, 10,
    48, 50, 55
Gram-stained bacteria, 58

Hatfield, Marcus, 21
headaches and whooping
    cough, 16
heme uptake, 47
hemoglobin, 33, 36

hemolysins, 48
hepatitis B, 70
H5N1. *See* avian influenza
    A
histamine, 49
HIV. *See* human immuno-
    deficiency virus
human immunodeficiency
    virus (HIV), 52–53
HurI, 47
HurR, 47

IgA. *See*
    immunoglobulin, A
IgG. *See*
    immunoglobulin, G
IgM. *See*
    immunoglobulin, M
immune system, 10, 37–44,
    72–73
immunoglobulin
    A (IgA), 39, 40
    G (IgG), 39
    M (IgM), 39
incubation stage, 29–30
Infantrix, 70. *See also*
    vaccination

infants, 9–10, 14, 15, 17, 37,
    68, 77, 81
infectious disease, 6–7, 8
influenza, 63, 79
inhalers, 79. *See also*
    vaccination
innate immune response,
    37, 38
iron, 33, 47

Kendrick, Pearl, 23–24,
    25, 70
kink, 19. *See also* whooping
    cough

Labrus ossifagus (cuckoo
    wrasse), 62
leprosy, 6
lipopolysaccharide, 35,
    48, 55

United States Food and
Drug Administration,
26
University of California–
Los Angeles, 46
University of California–
Santa Barbara, 43
University of Cincinnati, 64

vaccination, 6
acellular vaccine, 26, 40,
70–71, 77, 86, 89
administering, 79
adolescents, 9, 13
adults, 9–10
compensation for injury,
75–78
contraindications, 74
current research, 78–80
deaths from, 75
early efforts, 23–26
effectiveness, 78
effect on *B. pertussis*
strains, 85–86
immune response, 39
improvements in, 23–24,
53
infants, 9–10, 14
lack of — in conflict
zones, 83
oral, 79

pertussis in vaccinated
people, 84–85
in prevention of whoop-
ing cough, 67–83
protection from, 71–73
rates, 12
safety, 75, 88–89
side effects, 73–74, 75
strategies, 80–81, 83
whole cell vaccine, 68–69,
71–72, 78
Vaccine Adverse Events
Reporting System
(VAERS), 75
vaccine potency test, 24
VAERS. *See* Vaccine
Adverse Events
Reporting System
Vanderbilt University, 84
vCJD. *See* Creutzfeldt-Jakob
disease
virulence factors, 33–37,
45–47, 85
vomiting, 27, 30

whiskey, 27. *See also*
whooping cough,
treatments
white blood cells, 40, 49–50
whole cell vaccine. *See* vaccination, whole cell vaccine

whooping cough
animal models of,
44–45
biology of, 29–47. *See also*
Bordetella pertussis
cases by age group, 14
cause of, 8–12, 20–26. *See
also Bordetella pertussis*
conditions confused with,
62–63
in conflict zones, 82
cost of treating, 65
death from, 12, 14–15, 17,
67–68, 82
described, 8–17
diagnosis, 13, 56–63
epidemiology, 12–13
future prospects, 88–89
history of, 18–28
prevention of, 67–83. *See
also* vaccination
stages of, 29–30
symptoms, 8–9
transmission of, 10,
30–32
treatments, 26–28, 64–66
wolfshusten, 19. *See also*
whooping cough

Zithromax. *See*
azithromycin

About the Author

Patrick Guilfoile earned his Ph.D. in Bacteriology from the University of Wisconsin-Madison. He subsequently did postdoctoral research at the Whitehead Institute for Biomedical Research at the Massachusetts Institute of Technology. He is a professor of biology at Bemidji State University in northern Minnesota, where he has taught Microbiology and Medical Microbiology, and is currently an Associate Vice President at the University. His most recent laboratory research focused on ticks and tick-borne bacterial diseases. He has authored or co-authored more than 20 papers in scientific and biology education journals. He has also written four books in the Deadly Diseases and Epidemics series (*Antibiotic-Resistant Bacteria*, *Tetanus*, *Diphtheria*, and *Chicken Pox*), a molecular biology laboratory manual, and a book on controlling the ticks that transmit Lyme disease.

About the Consulting Editor

Hilary Babcock, M.D., M.P.H., is an assistant professor of Medicine at Washington University School of Medicine at Washington University School of Medicine and the Medical Director of Occupational Health for Barnes-Jewish Hospital and St. Louis Children's Hospital. She received her undergraduate degree from Brown University and her M.D. from the University of Texas Southwestern Medical Center at Dallas. After completing her residency, chief residency, and Infectious Disease fellowship at Barnes-Jewish Hospital, she joined the faculty of the Infectious Disease division. She completed an M.P.H. in Public Health from St. Louis University School of Public Health in 2006. She has lectured, taught, and written extensively about infectious diseases, their treatment, and their prevention. She is a member of numerous medical associations and is board certified in infectious disease. She lives in St. Louis, Missouri.